DWIGHT HOWE

THE CROWD

Decoding the Dynamics of
Collective Human Behavior
(2024 Beginner's Guide)

Copyright © 2024 by Dwight Howe

All rights reserved. No part of this publication may be reproduced, stored or transmitted in any form or by any means, electronic, mechanical, photocopying, recording, scanning, or otherwise without written permission from the publisher. It is illegal to copy this book, post it to a website, or distribute it by any other means without permission.

First edition

This book was professionally typeset on Reedsy.
Find out more at reedsy.com

Contents

1 Preface	1
2 Chapter I.	11
3 Chapter II.	18
4 Chapter III.	31
5 Chapter IV.	39
6 Chapter I.	44
7 Chapter II.	56
8 Chapter III.	64
9 Chapter IV.	80
10 Chapter I.	90
11 Chapter II.	94
12 Chapter III.	99
13 Chapter IV.	104
14 Chapter V.	110

1

Preface

The description of crowd features is the focus of the work that follows.

The collective traits that people of a race inherit from their ancestors make up the race's genius. On the other hand, observation demonstrates that when a specific number of these people are brought together in a crowd for purposes of action, specific new psychological traits emerge from their mere presence, which are added to the racial traits and occasionally diverge greatly from them.

Although organized crowds have always been significant in people's lives, their role has never been more significant than it is now. One of the main features of the modern era is the replacement of individual conscious activity by the collective unconsciousness of crowds.

I have made an effort to approach the challenging issue raised by the masses in a purely scientific manner, meaning that I have tried to follow a methodical approach free from the influence of beliefs, theories, or doctrines. This, in my opinion, is the only way to find a few bits of truth, particularly when dealing with a topic like this one that is the focus of fervent debate.

However, I should still explain to the reader why I have drawn conclusions from my research that may not initially seem to support them. For example, even though I have noted the extreme mental inferiority of crowds — including selected assemblies — I still maintain that meddling with their organization would be dangerous.

The reason is that, despite social organisms being as bit as complex as other species, it is not within our ability to force them to go through abrupt, drastic modifications. This is something that even the most careful observation of historical facts has consistently shown me. Nature occasionally employs drastic methods, but it never follows our style, which is why it is.

The study of social phenomena is inextricably linked to the study of the populations from whom they originate. Philosophically speaking, these phenomena might have an absolute value, but in reality, they only have a relative value.

As a result, when researching a social phenomenon, it is imperative to examine it from two distinct angles in turn. Then, it will become clear that practical reason and pure reason's teachings frequently conflict. Hardly any kind of data — physical or otherwise — is unaffected by this divide. In terms of absolute truth, a cube and a circle are geometric forms that are invariant and precisely specified by specific formulas.

When studying social phenomena, philosophers should keep in mind that these phenomena also have a practical value, and that this value is the only one that matters in terms of how civilization has evolved. He should be extremely cautious about the conclusions that reasoning would initially seem to force upon him as a result of realizing this reality.

He is required to have a similar reserve for various reasons.

PREFACE

Social facts are so complicated that it is hard to understand them all at once or to predict how their mutual influence will manifest itself. It appears that thousands of invisible causes can occasionally be concealed underneath the obvious facts.

Undoubtedly, crowds are inherently unconscious; nonetheless, it's possible that this very unawareness contributes to their power. In the natural world, creatures that are solely driven by instinct carry out astonishingly sophisticated actions. The ability to reason is a relatively new and imperfect human quality that cannot fully reveal the unconscious' rules to us, and cannot fully replace it. The unconscious has a huge influence on all of our actions, while reason has a very minor one. The unconscious functions as an unidentified energy.

Therefore, if we want to stay inside the safe but limited parameters that science may use to get knowledge and avoid straying into the realm of speculative thinking and false hypothesis,

Introduction.

The Era of Crowds

The development of the modern era — Modern belief in the power of crowds — The significant changes in national thought that have resulted in significant changes in civilizationIt modifies the conventional policies of the European states; explains the origins of the popular classes and how they wield their influence; outlines the inevitable fallout from the crowd's power; and illustrates how crowds are unable of acting in any other way than a destructive manner.The masses are the ones responsible for the breakdown of aging civilizations. — A general lack of understanding of crowd psychology — The significance of crowd research for politicians and leaders.

At first glance, it appears that political changes have a greater influence on the huge upheavals that precede the collapse of civilizations like the Roman Empire and the establishment of the Arabian Empire.

This age is one of those pivotal times when human thought is becoming more diverse.

This transition is based on two essential principles. The first is the deconstruction of the social, political, and religious ideologies that serve as the foundation for every aspect of our civilization. The second is the consequence of contemporary scientific and industrial discoveries, which is the formation of completely new circumstances of existence and thought.

The modern era is characterized by a period of transition and anarchy, with the concepts of the past remaining potent despite being partially destroyed and the ideas that will replace them still forming. It is difficult to predict now what will evolve in the future.

Hardly a century ago, the main forces influencing events were the rivalry between sovereigns and the conventional policies of European states. Public opinion was rarely taken into consideration, and oftentimes it was not taken into consideration at all. The customs that once governed politics, as well as the personal inclinations and rivalries of the ruling class, are no longer relevant; instead, the voice of the people has taken center stage. Kings listen to this voice, which commands them how to behave, and they make an effort to do what it says. These days, the hearts of the people determine a nation's destiny rather than the councils of kings.

One of the most notable aspects of our period of transition is the popular classes' entry into politics, or more accurately, their gradual transformation into the ruling classes. The defining characteristic of this transfer of political power is not, as might be assumed, the establishment of universal suffrage, which had a significant impact for a considerable amount of time. The dissemination of some ideas that have gradually crept into people's consciousness has contributed to the power of the masses to increase over time. More recently, the gradual coming together of people who are committed to bringing theoretical concepts to reality has done the same. Crowds have arrived to the acquisition of concepts pertaining to their well-defined interests through association.

The mass's demands of today are becoming more and more clearly defined, and they amount to nothing less than a will to completely destroy society as it currently exists in order to return it to the primitive communism that all human groups lived under prior to the dawn of civilization. These include restrictions on work hours, nationalization of mines, railroads, factories, and the land, equitable product distribution, the abolition of the top classes for the benefit of the lower classes, and so forth.

Crowds, however, are not well suited to reason and move quickly. Their current organization has greatly increased their strength.

In order to combat the disorder in men's minds, these writers — who enjoy the favor of our middle classes and best represent their narrow ideas, somewhat prescribed views, superficial skepticism, and occasionally excessive egoism — display profound alarm at this new power that they see growing. They are also making depressing appeals to those moral forces of the Church that they previously professed to detest. They remind us of the principles of revealed truth, speak to us about the fallacy of science, and travel back to Rome in penance. These recent converts don't realize it's too late. If grace had truly touched them, such an operation could not have had the same impact on less concerned minds.

Science has never been bankrupt, nor has it contributed to the current state of intellectual disorder or to the emergence of the new power that is emerging within it. Science never promised us bliss or serenity; all it ever offered was truth, or at least an understanding of such relations that our brain could grasp. It is deaf to our cries and sovereignly unaffected by our emotions. Since nothing can restore the illusions that science has demolished, it is our responsibility to make an effort to coexist with it.

Worldwide signs that are evident in every country demonstrate the strength of crowds expanding quickly and refute our belief that it will eventually stop developing.

The most evident mission of the masses has been to destroy a worn-out civilization completely up to this point. It's not just that this can be traced now, though. History teaches us that those violent and unconscious masses known, quite rightly, as barbarians, are ultimately responsible for the disintegration of civilizations, starting from the point at which the moral principles upon which they erred have lost their potency. To date, crowds have never produced or led a civilization; instead, it has always been a small, intellectual aristocracy. The only thing a crowd is good for is devastation. Every period of their rule is essentially a barbaric one. A civilization consists of all of the following: rigid laws, order, transitioning from an instinctual to a rational state, planning for the future, and a high level of culture.

Is our civilization destined for the same end? Although there is reason to believe that this is the case, we are not yet in a position to know for sure.

Whatever the case, we have no choice but to accept the rule of the masses as every barrier that could have held the mob in check has been overthrown by a lack of vision.

We barely know anything about these crowds, which are starting to generate a lot of talk. Professional psychology students have always disregarded them since they have lived far away from them, and the few times they have recently focused on this topic, it has only been to examine the crimes that crowds are capable of.

All of the world's masters, including the founders of empires and religions, eminent statesmen, apostles of all beliefs, and, in a more humble capacity, simple chiefs of small groups of men, have actually always been unconscious psychologists with an innate and frequently very certain understanding of the nature of crowds. It is this accurate understanding of this nature that has allowed them to establish their mastery with such ease. Napoleon had a remarkable understanding of the psychology of the masses in the nation he ruled, but occasionally he misinterpreted the psychology of crowds made up of people of different races.[1] It is as a result of this misinterpretation that he participated in the following actions in Spain, most notably in Russia:

The simplest example is the one that comes before. Its appropriateness will be apparent to all. Napoleon, being a psychologist, was aware of it, but modern legislators, who are unaware of the traits of a population, are unable to see its value. They still haven't learned enough from experience to believe that men's behavior is always determined by the principles of pure reason.

The psychology of crowds may have many more useful applications. Understanding this science provides the most vivid light on a wide range of historical and economic processes that would otherwise be completely unfathomable. I will have the opportunity to demonstrate why Taine, the most amazing modern historian, has occasionally written so erroneously.

Therefore, even just from a practical standpoint, it was worthwhile to try studying the psychology of crowds. Even if its interest stemmed solely from curiosity, it would still be worthy of consideration. Understanding the motivations behind human behavior is just as fascinating as learning the properties of a plant or mineral. Our analysis of the genius of crowds can only be a succinct synthesis or an outline of our research.

It just needs a few provocative views, nothing more. Some will cover the ground more extensively than me. We have merely scratched the surface of this nearly unspoiled land today.

Book I.

The Mind of Crowds

Chapter I.

General Characteristics of Crowds.—

Psychological Law of Their Mental Unity.

From a psychological perspective, what makes up a crowd is— Even a sizable group of people is insufficient to constitute a crowd. Particular traits of psychological crowds include: the ideas and sentiments of the people who make up the crowd turning in a fixed direction and the disappearance of their personalities; the crowd is always dominated by unconscious considerations; the disappearance of brain activity and the predominance of medullar activity; the lowering of intelligence and the total transformation of sentiments The altered feelings could be more favorable or unfavorable than those of the people that make up the crowd. You can be just as heroic or criminal in a crowd.

The term "crowd" refers to a collection of people, regardless of their ethnicity, occupation, or sexual orientation, as well as the circumstances that may have led them to be together. When seen from a psychological perspective, the word "crowd" takes on a very different meaning. Only in specific situations may an assortment of men exhibit new traits that are significantly distinct from those of the individuals that make up the group. Every individual in the assembly has the same thoughts and feelings, and their individuality becomes less apparent. A communal mind is created, one that is undoubtedly fleeting yet has extremely distinct qualities. Thus, the assembly has evolved into what I would refer to as an organized crowd, if there is a better phrase for it.

It is clear that a group of people do not automatically take on the characteristics of an organized crowd just because they happen to be seated next to each other. A thousand people who happened to congregate in a public area without a prearranged purpose is by no means a throng from a psychological perspective. It takes the effect of certain predisposing causes — the nature of which we must ascertain — for such a throng to take on its unique qualities.

The key features of a crowd preparing to become organised are the absence of conscious personality and the redirection of feelings and thoughts in a certain direction. However, these traits are not necessarily accompanied by the simultaneous presence of many people in one place. Thousands of solitary people may develop the traits of a psychological crowd at specific times when they are affected by specific violent emotions — like, say, a major national event. In that instance, it will be sufficient for their acts to instantly take on the qualities distinctive to the acts of a crowd simply by happenstance. Half a dozen guys may occasionally form a psychological crowd, although this may not occur when there are hundreds.

CHAPTER I.

Once assembled, a psychological mob takes on certain definite yet temporary general characteristics. Specific features that differ based on the crowd's constituent parts and have the potential to alter its mental composition are adjacent to these broad characteristics. Therefore, psychological crowds can be classified. As we study this topic, we will find that heterogeneous crowds — that is, crowds made up of dissimilar elements — present certain characteristics in common with homogeneous crowds, that is, crowds made up of elements that are somewhat similar (sects, castes, and classes), and that these common characteristics are accompanied by particularities that allow the two types of crowds to be distinguished from one another.

However, before we get too caught up in the many types of crowds, let's take a closer look at the traits that they all share. We will begin our work in the same manner as the naturalist, who first describes the generic traits shared by every member of a family before focusing on the specific traits that enable the differentiation of the genera and species that the family comprises.

It is challenging to accurately characterize the thinking of crowds due to the fact that their organization differs depending on factors such as race, composition, and the type and intensity of stimulating events that they are exposed to. But the same challenge arises when examining an individual's psychological data. It is exclusively in novels that people.

Since it is impossible to examine every level of crowd organization in this space, we will focus mostly on those crowds that have reached the stage of full organization. We will witness what crowds can become in this fashion, but not what they always are. Only in this advanced stage of organization are some new and distinct traits imposed on the homogeneous and dominant character of the race; only then does the already mentioned turning of all the collectivity's emotions and thoughts in one direction occur. Only in these types of situations does the psychological law of the mental oneness of crowds — which I mentioned earlier — come into effect.

The following is the most notable oddity that a psychological crowd presents: No matter how different each person is from the others in terms of intelligence, character, mode of life, or occupation, what unites them is that their transformation into a crowd gives them a collective mind that influences how they feel, think, and behave, which is very different from how each person would behave if they were alone. There are some thoughts and emotions that, aside from people coming together to create a crowd, do not materialize or manifest into acts. The psychological mob is a transient entity made up of diverse.

It is simple to demonstrate the differences between an isolated person and a member of a crowd, but it is more difficult to identify the reasons behind these differences.

In order to at least catch a glimpse of them, it is first required to remember the reality established by contemporary psychology, which holds that unconscious phenomena significantly influence both the functioning of intelligence and organic existence. The mind's unconscious existence is far more significant than its conscious existence.

Even the most perceptive analyst and keen observer rarely uncovers more than a handful of the unconscious motivations guiding their behavior.

All members of a race are more alike when it comes to the unconscious qualities that make up that race's genius; in contrast, the main areas where members of that race diverge from one another are the conscious qualities of their personalities, which are primarily the result of exceptional inherited circumstances and education. Even while men and women differ greatly in terms of IQ, they yet share many instincts, desires, and emotions. The most notable men seldom ever go above and beyond the norm when it comes to everything that falls under the category of feeling, including politics, religion, morality, affections, and antipathies. There can be a chasm of knowledge between a brilliant mathematician and his boot maker, yet.

These general character traits, which are mostly determined by unconscious processes and shared to a similar extent by most normal members of a race, are what I mean when I say that in crowds, these traits become common property. Individuals' intellectual prowess and, hence, their uniqueness are diminished in the common consciousness. The homogeneity overwhelms the heterogeneity, giving the unconscious traits the upper hand.

The reason crowds are incapable of performing tasks requiring a high level of intelligence is because they have common ordinary features. An assembly of distinguished individuals who are experts in several fields makes decisions pertaining to topics of public interest, but they are not.

A crowd's members would only be striking an average rather than creating new features, which is actually the case, as we have shown, if they limited themselves to sharing the common traits that each member of the group possesses. In what way are these novel traits generated? It is this that we are going to look into now.

These peculiar qualities that are peculiar to groups and not held by lone individuals develop for various reasons. The first is that a person in a crowd feels like he has unstoppable power because of his sheer numbers, which enables him to give in to instincts that he would have had to suppress if he had been alone.

It is important to keep in mind a few recent physiological discoveries in order to comprehend this phenomenon. We now know that a person may be made unconscious through a variety of means, to the point where, once completely devoid of consciousness, he follows the operator's instructions and behaves in ways completely at odds with his habits and character. The most meticulous observations seem to demonstrate that someone who spends some time immersed in a crowd of people going about their business quickly finds himself in a unique state that closely resembles the state of fascination in which the hypnotized person finds himself, either as a result of the crowd's magnetic influence or for some other reason that we are unaware of.

This is also roughly how it is for the person who belongs to a psychological crowd. He is no longer aware of what he is doing. Similar to the hypnotized person, in his situation, certain faculties may be severely diminished while others may be greatly elevated. He will behave irresistibly impetuously when under the impact of a proposal, carrying out certain tasks. Because the suggestion is the same for every member of the crowd, its impetuosity is stronger through reciprocity, making it more irresistible in the case of crowds than in the case of the hypnotized person. The individuals inside the group who could have a strong enough personality to withstand.

In addition, a guy moves down the social hierarchy only by belonging to a structured group of people. In solitude, he might be a refined person; in a throng, he is a barbarian, an instinctive creature. He has the spontaneity, violence, ferocity, enthusiasm, and heroism of primitive beings, whom he also tends to resemble by the ease with which he permits himself to

CHAPTER I.

be moved by words and images, which would have no effect whatsoever on each of the solitary people that make up the crowd, and to be persuaded to do actions that run counter to his most evident passions and well-established routines. In a crowd, an individual is like a grain of sand amidst other grains.

The preceding information leads to the conclusion that while the solitary individual is always intellectually superior to the crowd, the crowd may occasionally be superior than the individual in terms of sentiments and the actions these feelings elicit. Everything is dependent on the type of suggestion that the throng is exposed to. It is this aspect that writers who have solely examined crowds from a criminal perspective have entirely missed. Undoubtedly, a mob may be both criminal and heroic at the same time. Instead of lone individuals, crowds can be persuaded to take a fatal risk in order to ensure the success of a belief or an idea.

3

Chapter II.

The Sentiments and Morality of Crowds

1. The impatience, impulsivity, and movement of crowds. The throng is susceptible to all externally stimulating factors and

reflects their ceaseless fluctuations. Crowds lack premeditation; their emotions are so overwhelming that they destroy any sense of personal interest; and they are influenced by race. 2. People in crowds are gullible and easily swayed by suggestions. Crowds are obedient to suggestions; they accept the mental images that are conjured up in their minds as genuine; and they all share the same mental images. — In a crowd, the uneducated man and the knowledgeable man are equal —

Some instances of the delusions that people in a crowd can fall victim to include: The inability to accept the evidence of large crowds — The consensus of multiple witnesses is one.

Now that the main characteristics of crowds have been broadly mentioned, a more in-depth analysis of these traits is needed.

It will be noted that among the unique traits of crowds are a number of traits that are almost always found in creatures from lower evolutionary orders, such as women, savages, and children. These traits include impulsivity, irritability, the inability to reason, the lack of judgment and the critical spirit, the exaggeration of emotions, and others. But I only mention this analogy in passing; my book does not include its demonstration. Furthermore, it would be of little value to individuals who are familiar with the psychology of apes, and it would hardly convince those who are not.

1. Impulsiveness, Mobility, and Irritability of Crowds.

When examining the basic traits of a crowd, we found that nearly all of its motivations are unconscious. The spinal cord has a lot greater impact over its actions than the brain. Crowds are similar to very primitive beings in this regard. Even though the acts are perfectly executed, because the brain is not involved in their execution, the person behaves as the stimulating stimuli to which he is subjected may decide. A crowd is influenced by everything that is exciting and outside of itself, and it reflects these constant changes. It is a slave to the impulses that are given to it. The solitary person could be exposed to the same fascinating factors as.

Crowds follow various impulses that can be cruel or generous, brave or timid, depending on their thrilling causes, but they are always so powerful that the interests of the individual, even those of self-preservation, never really matter. Because there are so many fascinating factors that might influence crowds and because they constantly follow orders, crowds are very movable. This explains how we witness them go from the most ferocious and murderous to the most extraordinary acts of charity and bravery in an instant. The role of an executioner can be played by a mob with ease, just as easily as that of a martyr. The bloody avalanches necessary for the victory of all beliefs have been provided by crowds.

A crowd is more than just impetuous and fluid. It is unwilling to acknowledge that anything could stand in the way of its want being fulfilled, much like a savage. Due to the sense of unstoppable power bestowed upon it by its sheer numbers, it is the less able to comprehend such an intervention. In a crowd, the idea of impossibility vanishes for the individual. An lonely person is well aware that he cannot burn down a palace or plunder a store on his own, and if he is inclined to do so, he will easily resist the urge. Joining a crowd, he is aware of the power that comes with size, and it is enough to inspire thoughts of murder.

1. **The Suggestibility and Credulity of Crowds.**

CHAPTER II.

We identified extreme suggestibility as one of the main features of crowds, and we have demonstrated the extent to which recommendations spread across any human gathering. This fact explains why the sentiments of a crowd can quickly shift in one way. A crowd is usually in a condition of expectant attention, no matter how indifferent they appear to be, which makes suggestion easy. The initial thought that occurs immediately becomes ingrained in everyone gathered's minds through a process of contagion, and the group's common thoughts quickly become reality.

The thought that has entered the brain tends to, as is the case with all people under the effect of suggestion,

Consequently, a group of people who are always on the verge of unconsciousness, easily swaying from suggestion to suggestion, and possessing the intense emotions unique to creatures devoid of critical thinking and incapable of appealing to reason, can only be overly credulous. The unlikely does not exist for a crowd, and this fact must be kept in mind in order to comprehend the ease with which the most unbelievable myths and tales are made and spread.3.

Their great credulity is not the only reason for the creation of the legends that circulate so freely in crowds. It is also the outcome of the enormous perversions that events go through in a crowd's mind.

The contagious suggestion begins with the initial distortion of the truth committed by one of the gathering's members. One of the people present very definitely saw St. George before he appeared to all the Crusaders on the walls of Jerusalem. Everyone instantly embraced the miracle that one individual had signaled through suggestion and virality.

This is always the working mechanism behind the mass

hallucinations that have occurred so often throughout history — hallucinations that, given that thousands of people have witnessed them, appear to bear all the hallmarks of authenticity.

The mental state of the individuals that make up a mob should not be taken into account in order to counter what came before. This attribute is unimportant. Both the learned man and the ignoramus are equally incapable of observation from the minute they join a crowd.

There may be a paradox in this thesis. It would be necessary to look into a lot of historical data in order to prove it beyond a reasonable doubt, and multiple books would not be enough.

However, in order to avoid giving the reader the impression that my claims are unfounded, I will provide him with a few examples that I have chosen at random from the countless others that could be cited.

The fact that follows is among the most common since it was selected from a group.

This example demonstrates the mechanism of a communal hallucination of the type we have described. The scene is composed of a crowd that is watching intently, on the one hand, and a watch signaling a crippled vessel at sea, on the other. The watch's advice was adopted by all those in attendance, including officers and sailors, through a process of infection.

It is not required for a crowd to be large in order for the ability to see what is happening in front of one's eyes to be shattered and for hallucinations unconnected to the actual facts to take their place. A crowd is formed as soon as a few people are gathered together, even though they should be well-known guys.

Numerous examples akin to this exist. The newspapers are replete with accounts of two young girls who were discovered

CHAPTER II.

drowned in the Seine as I type these words. First and foremost, six witnesses were able to identify these kids with the utmost clarity. The juge d'instruction was undoubtedly still thinking about all the affirmations because they were in such complete correspondence.

He had the death certificate prepared, but right before the children were set to be buried, it was discovered by pure happenstance that the alleged victims were still alive and bore only a passing similarity to the drowned girls.

Something amazing happened. "Good Heavens, it's my child!" cried a widow the day after a pupil identified the corpse."After being brought up to the body, she looked over the clothes and saw a scar on the forehead. "It's definitely my son who vanished last July," she affirmed. He has been killed and taken from me."The woman, Chavandret, worked as the Rue du Four's concierge. When questioned, her brother-in-law stated, "That is the little Filibert," after being called. A number of bystanders identified the boy discovered near La Villette as Filibert Chavandret, including the boy's schoolmaster, who made the identification based on a medal the youngster was wearing.

It will be noted that women and children, who are the most impressionable individuals, are the ones who typically make these recognitions. They simultaneously demonstrate to us the value that these witnesses have in legal proceedings. Statements made by youngsters, in particular, should never be used against them. Magistrates frequently assert that youngsters are not dishonest. If they had a somewhat more developed psychological culture than what is actually the case, they would be aware that youngsters always lie — lie after all, even if it's an innocent one. Tossing a coin to determine an accused person's destiny would be preferable to, as.

Sadly, legends lack consistency in and of themselves, despite the fact that books have unquestionably documented them. Because of the passage of time and, more importantly, racial factors, the crowd's imagination constantly changes them. The God of Love of Sainte Therese and the bloodthirsty Jehovah of the Old Testament are poles apart, and the Buddhas that are worshipped in China and India are very different from one another.

It's not even essential for heroes to exist in a different era from our own for the collective imagination to alter their legend. Occasionally, the change happens in a matter of years.

1. **The Exaggeration and Ingenuousness of the Sentiments of Crowds.**

Whether a crowd is expressing positive or negative emotions, they always have the same dual nature: they are both extremely basic and extremely dramatic. An person in a crowd has a lot in common with prehistoric creatures, both on this and many other points.

He perceives things as a whole and is unaware of their intermediary stages since he is incapable of making subtle distinctions. Any feeling, once it is expressed, communicates itself extremely fast by a process of suggestion and contagion, and the obvious approval of which it is the object significantly increases its force. This causes the sentiments of a crowd to be exaggerated.

Crowds are known for their simplicity and amplification of emotions, which leaves them devoid of ambiguity or confusion.

The lack of any sense of accountability also contributes to the violence of crowd emotions, particularly in diverse crowds.

CHAPTER II.

In the event of crowd feelings and actions, the thought of a significant temporary force due to number and the certainty of impunity, which grows stronger with crowd size, make it impossible for the solitary individual. The idea of violent, fleeting, but great strength takes over the dumb, ignorant, and jealous people in crowds, freeing them from their sense of insignificance and helplessness. Unfortunately, negative emotions are sometimes exacerbated by the exaggeration inclination of crowds.

A crowd that is prone to hyperbole will only find greatness in extreme emotions. A speaker who wants to impact a gathering must utilize aggressive affirmations abusively. Speakers at public gatherings are well familiar with the following strategies of argumentation: exaggeration, affirmation, repetition, and never attempting to prove anything by reasoning.

Furthermore, a crowd tends to exaggerate the feelings it has for their heroes. It is necessary to continuously exaggerate their perceived virtues and qualities. It has been rightly observed that a public on stage expects a level of bravery, integrity, and virtue from the piece's hero that is never found in real life.

It is entirely appropriate that emphasis has been placed on the unique perspective that theater provides on many issues. There is undoubtedly such a viewpoint, but most of the time its principles have nothing to do with logic or common sense. Undoubtedly, the skill of captivating large crowds is of a lower caliber, but it does require certain unique abilities. Reading plays makes it difficult to understand why they are successful. Theater managers are typically apprehensive about a piece's chances of success when they accept it since they need to be able to pass for a crowd in order to assess the material.Six If we were able to go into further detail here, we would once again demonstrate the overwhelming impact.

It goes without saying that people only prefer to exaggerate in situations involving sentiments and not intelligence at all when they are in a crowd.

As I've already demonstrated, a person's intellectual standards are immediately and significantly reduced just by being a part of a crowd.

This truth has also been confirmed by erudite magistrate M. Tarde in his studies on crimes involving crowds. Crowds can only surge to an extremely high or, conversely, fall to an extremely low level in relation to sentiment.

1. **The Intolerance, Dictatorialness and Conservatism of Crowds.**

The thoughts, ideas, and beliefs that are presented to a crowd are either accepted or rejected collectively and are seen as either absolute truths or equally extreme errors. Crowds are only aware of basic and extreme emotions. This is consistently the case when beliefs are generated by suggestion rather than logic. Everyone is aware of the oppressive empire that religious ideas impose on people's brains, as well as the bigotry that goes along with them.

A crowd is both intolerant and inclined to grant authority to its inspirations because it lacks clarity over what defines truth and error, but it also has a strong sense of its own power. A crowd will never accept disagreement and debate; an individual may.

All types of crowds experience some degree of dictatorialism and intolerance, albeit to differing degrees. This is where the core idea of race that permeates all of men's emotions and thinking reared its head again. The highest levels of authoritarianism and intolerance are found among Latino populations in particular. As a matter of fact, their growth among Latino masses has completely undermined the Anglo-Saxon notion of the individual's authority and freedom. The urge that they feel to bring people who disagree with them together characterizes the Latino crowd's sense of independence, which is limited to the collective independence of the sect to which they belong. Crowds are highly susceptible to the notions of authoritativeness and intolerance, which they readily imagine, entertain, and, when imposed upon them, effortlessly put into practice.

Crowds are passive in their reverence for force and only mildly moved by kindness, which they view as nothing more than a sign of weakness. Their sympathies have always been reserved for despots who brutally persecuted them rather than for relaxed masters. They constantly erect the tallest statues in honor of these latter. It is true that they voluntarily crush the despot they have overthrown, but this is because, having lost strength, he has returned to the ranks of the weak, who are to be subjugated.

A mob is always willing to rise up against the weak and submit to a powerful ruler. If the power of an authority is erratic, the populace alternates between anarchy and slavery and between servitude and anarchy because it is constantly submissive to its strong emotions.

But it would be a complete misinterpretation of their nature to think that revolutionary inclinations predominate in crowds. Their inclination towards violence is what misleads us in this regard. Their violent and disobedient outbursts are never lasting. Crowds are too heavily influenced by unconscious factors and too susceptible to secular inherited influences to be extremely conservative. Left on their own, they quickly grow tired of chaos and automatically resort to slavery.

Understanding history, and popular revolutions in particular, becomes challenging if the deeply conservative tendencies of masses are not adequately taken into consideration. It is true that they want to rename their institutions, and they occasionally even carry out violent revolutions to achieve this goal, but the fundamental nature of these institutions is too strongly an expression of the racial needs for them to consistently deviate from it. Their constant movement only has an impact on very superficial issues. Indeed, their conservative tendencies are as strong as those of any prehistoric creature. They have an unwavering, fetishistic reverence for all traditions, and they secretly detest any innovation that could alter the fundamentals.

1. **The Morality of Crowds.**

If one interprets "morality" as the unwavering observance of specific social norms and the ongoing suppression of one's own desires, then it is obvious that crowds are too impetuous and too movable to be moral. On the other hand, we may argue that crowds occasionally display extremely high moral standards if we define morality to encompass the fleeting manifestation of traits like selflessness, devotion, disinterest, abnegation, and the demand for equity.

The few psychologists who have examined crowds exclusively from the perspective of their illegal behavior have concluded that crowds have very low moral standards after observing how frequently these behaviors occur. This is undoubtedly the case frequently, but why?

While a crowd is capable of much higher deeds than an isolated individual, such as acts of sacrifice, dedication, and apathy, it may also be guilty of murder, incendiarism, and other crimes of all kinds. Appealing to feelings of pride, honor, and patriotism has the potential to greatly impact an individual who is a part of a crowd, sometimes even to the point of sacrificing their own life. There are many historical examples that are similar to the ones provided by the volunteers in 1793 and the Crusaders. Only collectives possess the capacity for both extreme dedication and apathy. How many people have bravely risked their lives for words, concepts, and ideals that they hardly understood?

It frequently happens that even total scoundrels are temporarily endowed with very rigid moral ideals just by virtue of their presence in a crowd. Taine draws attention to the fact that the perpetrators of the September killings placed diamonds and pocket books that they had discovered on their victims and could have easily taken with them when they placed them on the committees' table. When the ragged, wailing mob assaulted the Tuileries in 1848 during the revolution, they were unable to seize any of the objects that had shocked them, including a bread supply that would have lasted for several days.

This mass moralization of the person is undoubtedly not a constant; rather,

If crowds therefore frequently give way to baser impulses, they also occasionally serve as role models for morally high deeds. If disinterestedness, resignation, and unwavering dedication to a genuine or fictitious goal are moral virtues, then it can be argued that crowds frequently exhibit these qualities to a degree that even the most learned philosophers seldom achieve. They probably put them into practice unintentionally, but it doesn't really matter. We shouldn't be too hard on ourselves for the fact that crowds, in particular, follow instinctive decisions rather than using reason. It's likely that no civilization would have developed on our planet and humanity would not have a past if they had, in some circumstances, reasoned and considered their immediate interests.

Chapter III.

The Ideas, Reasoning Power, and Imagination of Crowds

The concepts of crowds. Basic and auxiliary conceptsThe social power of ideas is independent of the degree of truth they may contain. — How contradictory concepts may exist simultaneously. — The change that high ideas must undergo before they are accessible to crowds. 2. The ability of crowds to reason. thinking should not be applied to crowds since their thinking is always of a much lower degree and there is just a seeming sequence or analogy in the concepts they associate. 3. The notion of throngs. Strength of the crowd's imagination: People think in pictures, and these pictures build on one another without any kind of connection; People are particularly struck by the magnificent; Legends and the magnificent are the true cornerstones of civilization; Popular imagination has always been.

1. The Ideas of Crowds

In examining the role that ideas have in the development

CHAPTER III.

of nations in a previous article, we demonstrated that every civilization is the product of a limited number of core concepts that are rarely updated. We demonstrated how these concepts get ingrained in the brains of large groups of people, how challenging the process is, and the influence these concepts have after they are successfully implemented. Ultimately, we observed that significant historical upheavals typically stem from modifications to these core concepts. Having covered this topic in sufficient detail, I won't be going back to it at this time. Instead, I'll limit myself to speaking briefly about concepts that are understandable to large audiences.

The great underlying ideals that supported our fathers are eroding more and more in the modern era. They have completely lost their solidity, and the institutions that support them are now trembling violently. Many of the fleeting little concepts I have been discussing are produced every day, but only a small percentage of them appear to be full of life and have the potential to become dominant.

Regardless of the concepts presented to masses, their ability to truly impact them depends on them taking on a rigid, unwavering, and uncomplicated form. Then, they take the form of images, which are exclusively visible to the general public in this capacity.

This is not a crowd-specific phenomenon. It is seen in many isolated cases, not just in the situation of primitive creatures but in the case of all those — the ardent adherents of a religious faith, for example — who are similar to primitive beings in some aspect of their intelligence. In the case of educated Hindoos who were raised in our European colleges and have earned their degrees, I have noticed its peculiar existence. Several concepts from the West had been imposed on top of their fixed, innate social or inherited beliefs. The individual presenting in this manner had different concepts that each had their own unique accompaniment of acts or words, depending on the current circumstances.

Ideas frequently require the most extensive alterations before becoming popular since they are only available to large audiences after taking on a very basic form. We see how extensive the changes necessary to bring them down to the level of the intellect of crowds are, particularly when we are dealing with fairly lofty philosophical or scientific notions. These changes depend on the characteristics of the crowds or the race to which the masses belong, but they always have a demeaning and simplifying tendency. This clarifies the observation that, from a social perspective, there is actually very little such thing as an idea hierarchy — that is, concepts that are more or less elevated.

Furthermore, an idea's inherent value and hierarchical value are irrelevant from a social perspective. The consequences it creates are the important thing to take into account. It is undeniably true that neither the democratic concepts of the previous century nor the Christian ideas of the Middle Ages nor the modern social ideas are particularly high. Even if they can only be viewed as regrettable mistakes from a philosophical standpoint, their influence has been and will continue to be enormous, making them one of the most important variables influencing how states behave for a very long time.

An idea only becomes influential after undergoing the changes that make it appealing to large audiences. These changes will be covered in another section.

Because it cannot be assumed that a thought can produce effective action even on highly developed minds just because its validity has been established. It is easy to understand this reality by observing how little of an impact the majority of men are affected by the most obvious example. Even the most obvious evidence can be accepted by an educated person, but the convert's unconscious mind will swiftly revert to its initial beliefs. When you see him again in a few days, he will restate his previous points in precisely the same words. In actuality, he is influenced by past concepts that have developed into sentiments, and these concepts alone have the power.

It takes time for ideas to get ingrained in the brains of masses, but it also takes time for them to be eliminated. Crowds always lag behind knowledgeable individuals and philosophers by several generations when it comes to ideas because of this. Though the influence of the fundamental ideas I mentioned earlier is still very strong, statesmen are still obligated to govern based on principles they no longer believe to be true, even though they are well aware of the mixture of error present in them.

2. The Reasoning Power of Crowds

It is impossible to say with certainty that mobs lack reason or that reasoning should not have any effect on them.

But from a logical standpoint, the arguments they use and those that can persuade them are of such a low caliber that the only way to characterize them as thinking is by analogy. Similar to higher order thinking, the inferior reasoning of crowds is predicated on the association of concepts; nevertheless, the only apparent connections between the ideas connected by crowds are those of analogy or succession. Crowds think similarly to the Esquimaux, who deduce that glass, which is equally translucent, must melt in the mouth because they know from experience that ice, a transparent body,

The linkage of disparate objects with just an apparent connection between them and the quick generalization of specific instances are traits of crowd reasoning. These kinds of arguments are the ones that crowd control experts consistently bring up. These are the only debates that have the power to sway large groups of people. Since most people cannot understand a series of logical arguments, it is acceptable to claim that they are not capable of reasoning, reason incorrectly, or should not be swayed by reasoning. Sometimes one is surprised to learn how bad some speeches were despite the fact that the audiences they addressed were greatly impacted by them,

It would be unnecessary to add that the inability of masses to reason correctly inhibits them from exhibiting any sign of the critical spirit, that is, from being able to distinguish error from truth or form an accurate opinion on any subject. Crowd judgments are never decisions made after deliberation; rather, they are judgments imposed upon them. When it comes to this issue, there are a lot of people that stay at the level of a mob. The majority of males find it extremely difficult to establish unique beliefs based on their own thinking, which contributes to the ease with which some opinions gain widespread acceptance.

3. The Imagination of Crowds

Crowds possess a highly potent, highly active, and highly responsive figurative imagination, much like individuals lacking in reasoning ability. A person, an incident, or an accident can conjure up mental pictures in their minds that are nearly as realistic as the actual thing. Crowds resemble a sleeper to some extent, whose reason is temporarily stopped and so permits the arousal of extremely intense visions in his mind, images that would rapidly fade if they were subjected to the process of reflection. Crowds lack the concept of improbability because they are incapable of introspection or thinking; however, it

CHAPTER III.

should be highlighted that in general, crowds.

Since crowds can only think in pictures, they can only be moved by pictures. Only visuals have the power to frighten or captivate them and inspire action.

This is why theatrical depictions, when the image is presented in its most recognizable form, consistently have a profound effect on audiences. For the common people of ancient Rome, bread and extravagant performances were the ultimate source of happiness, and they demanded nothing more. Over the next centuries, this ideal has not changed. Nothing stimulates crowds' imaginations more than dramatic depictions, regardless of their demographic. The same emotions are felt simultaneously by the entire audience, and if these feelings do not immediately translate into acts,

The popular imagination serves as the foundation for the might of states and the might of conquerors. More specifically, crowds are directed by utilizing this imagination. All significant historical events, including the growth of Christianity, Islamism, Buddhism, the Reformation, the French Revolution, and, more recently, the frightening spread of socialism, are either directly or indirectly the result of powerful impressions made on the collective imagination of the populace.

Furthermore, all great leaders throughout history, especially the most totalitarian despots, have recognized the public imagination as the source of their authority and have never tried to rule against it. Napoleon declared to the Council of State, "It was by becoming a Catholic that I terminated.

How impressive is the imagination of the masses? We'll find out soon. For the time being, let's just agree that the achievement cannot be made by trying to improve the ability of reasoning or intelligence — that is, by way of demonstration.

By reciting Caesar's will aloud to the crowd and pointing to his corpse, Antony was able to mobilize the population against his killers without the use of crafty rhetoric. Anything that captures the interest of large groups usually takes the form of an astonishingly vivid picture that is devoid of any further context or just accompanied by a few amazing or enigmatic facts: As instances, consider a significant triumph,

Therefore, it is not the facts per se that capture the public's attention, but rather the manner in which they occur and are made public. It is imperative that they create a striking vision that overwhelms and consumes the mind by their condensation, if I may put it in that way. Understanding how to capture a crowd's imagination while also managing them is a skill in its own right.

Chapter IV.

A Religious Shape Assumed by All the Convictions of Crowds

What is meant by the religious sentiment? It is not dependent on the worship of a deity. Its attributes include the intensity of beliefs taking on a religious form.Popular gods have always existed; new forms under which they are resurrected; religious forms of atheism; the significance of these ideas from a historical perspective; The religious sentiments of large crowds, not the will of lone individuals, are what led to the Reformation, Saint Bartholomew, the Terror, and all similar occurrences.

We have demonstrated that mobs lack the ability to reason, that they either embrace or reject ideas in their entirety, that they cannot stand disagreement or debate, and that the ideas imposed upon them tend to invade every aspect of their awareness and quickly turn into acts. We have demonstrated that sufficiently influenced audiences are willing to give their lives in service of the goal that has inspired them. We have also shown that they only tolerate strong and intense emotions; in their case, pity turns into admiration very fast, and dislike turns into hatred nearly as soon as it is triggered. These broad indicators give us a glimpse into the nature of the beliefs held by large groups of people.

A person is not only religious when he worships a deity; rather, he is religious when he devotes all of his mental faculties, all of his will, and all of his soulful fervor to the service of a cause or a person who serves as the focal point and direction of his thoughts and deeds.

The religious mood must be accompanied by intolerance and extremism. Those who think they know the key to either temporary or permanent happiness will always exhibit them. When any form of conviction inspires a man, these two traits are present in all men combined. At its core, the Reign of Terror's Jacobins shared the same theological beliefs as the Inquisition's

CHAPTER IV.

Catholics,

Crowd convictions take on traits like ferocious intolerance, mindless obedience, and the necessity for aggressive propaganda that are intrinsic to religious sentiment; as a result, it is possible to say that all of their beliefs have a religious form. A mob's chosen hero is considered a god-like figure to that throng. For fifteen years Napoleon was such a god, and no deity ever had more ardent devotees or more easily sent men to their deaths. Never before have the gods of Christianity and Pagan mythology had such complete control over the brains that they had subjugated.

Every religious or political creed's founder created it because they were able to enthuse masses with the kind of extreme emotions that.

These superstitions are not something that science has definitively eliminated from the past. Reason and sentiment have always been at odds, and sentiment has never won. The terms "divinity" and "religion," in whose name they were held captive for so long, will no longer be spoken by crowds. However, in the past century, they have acquired an unprecedented number of fetishes, and the ancient deities have never had so many statues and altars erected in their honor. Individuals who have recently examined the popular movement dubbed "boulangism" have observed how easily the religious impulses of masses can be reawakened. A country inn could not exist that did not have the hero's image.

Therefore, it is a very pointless cliché to say that the people need a religion because all political, religious, and social creeds only get entrenched among them under the condition that they constantly adopt the religious form—a form that eliminates the possibility of debate. If it were possible to persuade the masses to become atheists, this belief would quickly take on the external trappings of a cult and display all the intolerance of a religious attitude. One odd example of this is the development of the little Positivist sect. The Positivists swiftly experienced what had happened to the Nihilist, whose tale is told by that deep thinker Dostoiewsky. One day, enlightened by reason, he smashed the images of the gods.

I'll say it again: some historical events, which are among the most significant, cannot be understood unless one has had a deep understanding of the religious form that the beliefs of the masses eventually take on. Certain social processes require significantly more investigation from a psychological perspective than from a naturalist one. Because the eminent historian Taine primarily examined the Revolution from a naturalist perspective, he has frequently missed the true origins of events. Although he has accurately noted the facts, he has not always been able to determine their origins because he has not studied the psychology of crowds.

The facts, with their ruthless, chaotic, and vicious nature, horrified him.

CHAPTER IV.

Book II.

The Opinions and Beliefs of Crowds

Chapter I.

Remote Factors of the Opinions and Beliefs of Crowds

Preparatory elements of crowd beliefs: The genesis of crowd beliefs results from an early elaboration process; examination

CHAPTER I.

of the many components of these beliefs. 1. Color. The dominant effect it possesses — It stands for the advice of the past. 2. Customs. Crowds are the most steadfast defenders of traditional views. They are the essence of the race. The social significance of customs. How once necessary, they become harmful. 3. The time. It sets up the formation of beliefs and their eventual demise one after the other. This element is necessary for order to emerge from chaos. 4. Institutions of politics and society.

They have a false impression of themselves; their impact is incredibly small; they are consequences rather than causes; and nations are unable to decide what seems to.

Having studied the mental constitution of crowds and become acquainted
with their modes of feeling, thinking, and reasoning, we shall now proceed
to examine how their opinions and beliefs arise and become established. The factors which determine these opinions and beliefs are of two
kinds: remote factors and immediate factors.

The remote factors are those which render crowds capable of adopting
certain convictions and absolutely refractory to the acceptance of others.

These factors prepare the ground in which are suddenly seen to germinate certain new ideas whose force and consequences are a cause of astonishment, though they are only spontaneous in appearance. The outburst and putting in practice of certain ideas among crowds present at times a startling suddenness. This is only a superficial effect, behind which must be sought a preliminary and preparatory action of long duration. The immediate factors are those which, coming on the top of this long, preparatory working, in whose absence they would remain without effect, serve as the source of active persuasion on crowds; that is, they are the factors which cause the idea to take shape and set it loose with all its consequences. The resolutions by which collectivities are suddenly carried

away arise out of these immediate factors; it is due to them that a riot breaks

out or a strike is decided upon, and to them that enormous majorities invest

one man with power to overthrow a government.

The successive action of these two kinds of factors is to be traced in all

great historical events. The French Revolution — to cite but one of the most striking of such events — had among its remote factors the writings of the philosophers, the exactions of the nobility, and the progress of scientific thought. The mind of the masses, thus prepared, was then easily roused by such immediate factors as the speeches of orators, and the resistance of the court party to insignificant reforms. Among the remote factors there are some of a general nature, which are found to underlie all the beliefs and opinions of crowds. They are race, traditions, time, institutions, and education. We now proceed to study the influence of these different factors.

1. Race

Race is a factor that has to be ranked first because it is significantly more important than all other factors combined. It is unnecessary to address it again because we have already covered it in sufficient detail in another book. In a previous volume, we defined historical races and explained how, once established, they have such power due to the laws of heredity that their institutions, beliefs, and artistic creations — in other words, every aspect of their civilization — are but the external manifestation of their innate brilliance. We demonstrated how the force of race is so great that no element can be transferred from one people to another without experiencing the deepest changes.

The current societal recommendations are reflected in the environment, circumstances, and occurrences.

2. Traditions

Traditions serve as a symbol for the beliefs, requirements, and emotions of the past.

They are the culmination of the race and have a tremendous influence over us.

Since embryology has demonstrated the enormous impact of the past on the evolution of living things, the biological sciences have undergone a significant transformation. The historical sciences will also experience a significant transformation as a result of the increasing acceptance of this idea. It is still not broad enough as of yet, and many statesmen are still no better than the thinkers of the previous century who thought that a society could break free from its past and completely reconstruct itself along lines given only by reason. A people are an organism that the past has formed, and much like any other organism,

It is not regrettable to be in this situation. Traditions are necessary for both civilization and the emergence of a national genius. As a result, since the beginning of time, man has been primarily concerned with creating a network of customs that he then seeks to eradicate once their advantageous benefits have worn off. Without traditions, civilization could not exist, and advancement could not occur without the eradication of those traditions. The challenge, and it is a great challenge, is to strike the right balance between stability and unpredictability. When a people's customs become too deeply ingrained, they become unchangeable and, similar to China, incapable of progressing. In this instance, violent revolutions are ineffective because either the shattered remnants.

Crowds are precisely those that resist change to established views the hardest and cling to them the most tightly. This is especially true for the group of people that make up castes. I've previously emphasized the conservative nature of crowds and demonstrated how even the most violent protests only result in a terminological shift. It may have seemed that the old religious beliefs had faded away at the end of the 20th century, when churches were destroyed and priests were banished or executed. However, only a few years had passed before the system of public worship that had been abolished had to be reinstated in obedience to widespread demands.

3. Time

Time is one of the most important and energetic aspects in both biological and social problems.

The only true creator and the only tremendous destroyer is it. Time is the force that has elevated the tiny cell of geological periods to human dignity and created mountains out of grains of sand. Centuries of action is all it takes to change any particular phenomenon. It's been accurately noted that an ant with enough time on its hands could completely flatten Mount Blanc. The power ascribed by believers to God would belong to an entity who could willfully change the course of time through magical force. Here, though, the only thing we need to worry about is how time shapes the origins of the opinions of the masses.

Time in especially prepares the ground for the thoughts and beliefs of crowds, or at the very least provides the soil upon which they will sprout. This explains why some concepts are feasible in one era but not in another. Time builds up the massive trash of ideas and beliefs that gives rise to the ideals of a particular era. Their roots are rooted in a long history; they do not sprout randomly or by accident. It is time that has prepared them for blooming when they do, and one must always look back into the past to get a sense of their origins. They are the mothers of today and the daughters of yesterday.

4. Political and Social Institutions

The notion that governments and institutions can strengthen one another, that institutions can correct societal flaws, and that decrees can bring about social change — all of these concepts are still widely held. It served as the impetus for the French Revolution and served as the foundation for contemporary social philosophies.

Even the most persistent experience hasn't been able to dispel this severe illusion. Historians and philosophers have tried in vain to refute it, but they have not had any trouble showing that institutions are products of ideas, feelings, and customs, and that laws do not have the power to change ideas, emotions, or customs. Institutions are not chosen by a country.

Furthermore, a people have no genuine ability to alter their institutions. It can surely change their name at the expense of bloody revolutions, but fundamentally they stay the same. The designations are only meaningless labels that a historian who investigates matters thoroughly hardly needs to worry about. In this sense, the most democratic nation in the world, England[9], yet maintains a monarchical government, whereas the Spanish-American Republics, despite having republican constitutions, are home to the most repressive dictatorship. Peoples' fortunes are shaped by their character, not by their government. In my earlier work, I tried to establish this viewpoint.

"To think nothing of symmetry and much of convenience; never to remove an anomaly merely because it is an anomaly; never to innovate except when some grievance is felt; never to innovate except so far as to get rid of the grievance; never to lay down any proposition of wider extent than the particular case for which it is necessary to provide; these are the rules which have, from the age of John to the age of Victoria, generally guided the deliberations of our two hundred and fifty Parliaments." The laws and institutions of each people would need to be examined one by one in order to demonstrate the extent to which they both express and fail to meet the needs of each race.

The inference that should be made from the foregoing is that institutions are not the best place to look for ways to significantly influence the collective genius of people. We must acknowledge that certain institutions are as alien to the greatness of one as they are to the decadence of the other when we observe that certain nations, like the United States, achieve a high degree of prosperity under democratic institutions while others, like the Spanish-American Republics, are found existing in a pitiful state of anarchy under absolutely similar institutions. People are ruled by their character, and any institutions that are not directly based on that character are only temporary masks that people wear.

1. Instruction and Education

The idea that education has the power to fundamentally alter people and would inevitably better and even equalize them is at the top of the list of prevalent ideas of the modern day.

This claim has ended up becoming one of the most enduring democratic dogmas just by virtue of its continual repetition.

CHAPTER I.

Attacking it would be just as challenging now as it was in the past when one was attacking church dogmas. Nonetheless, democratic theories profoundly conflict with the findings of psychology and experience on this, as well as many other points. Herbert Spencer is one of several notable philosophers who have little trouble demonstrating that education does not make a person more moral.

It is not a given that well-directed education won't have a positive practical impact, if not in the sense of elevating moral standards then at least in the sense of fostering professional capacity. However, no one has ever argued against this idea. Unfortunately, the peoples of Latin America have, particularly in the last 25 years, built their educational systems on extremely incorrect premises. Despite the observations of highly esteemed scholars, including Breal, Fustel de Coulanges, Taine, and numerous others, they continue to make these regrettable errors. In a piece that was published a while back, I personally demonstrated how the French educational system turns most of its graduates into social outcasts and creates a large following of adherents to the worst kinds.

If this education was completely pointless, all one could do would be to feel sorry for the sad little kids who attend elementary school learning about the ancestry of Clotaire's sons, the wars between Neustria and Austrasia, or the taxonomy of animals instead of doing important coursework. However, the system poses a much greater risk. Those who are subjected to it develop a strong aversion to the circumstances of their birth and a strong desire to leave it behind. The working class no longer wants to be working men, and the peasant no longer wants to be a peasant, while the lowest members of the middle class acknowledge that their sons have no other options for a career than becoming paid employees of the state.

The government, which creates all these diploma holders out of textbooks, can only employ a certain percentage of these people, forcing the others to go unemployed. As a result, it must accept that the others are its foes and that it must feed the previously stated. The professions are under attack from the top to the bottom of the social pyramid, from the most modest clerk to the professor and the prefect, due to the vast number of people who possess certificates. Thousands of applicants apply for the lowest official positions, yet a businessman has the hardest time hiring an agent to represent him in the colonies. In the Seine department alone, 20,000 schoolteachers and mistresses are unemployed.

Clearly, it is too late to turn back now. Only experience, the greatest teacher of all, will struggle to point out our error. It will be sufficient on its own to demonstrate the need for industrial education capable of compelling our young men to return to the fields, the workshop, and the colonial enterprise that they avoid today at all costs, in place of our repugnant textbooks and pitiful exams.

The professional training that our ancestors formerly received was the training that all enlightened minds are today demanding. It is still strong today among the countries that control the world by their initiative, drive, and spirit of enterprise.

Even though our classical education produced nothing but unhappy people and people unfit for their station in life, one might be willing to put up with all the drawbacks of it in a pinch. After all, did the mindless memorization of countless textbooks and superficial knowledge really increase intelligence? Does it, however, actually raise this bar? Unfortunately, no! The attributes of judgment, experience, initiative, and character —

qualities that cannot be acquired through reading — are prerequisites for success in life. Books are dictionaries, and while they are helpful to consult, it is completely pointless to keep large chunks of them in your memory.

How may professional education improve intelligence to such an extent that it surpasses.

Ideas, according to him, can only be formed in their natural and normal environments. The many sensory-pleasing impressions that a young man encounters on a daily basis in settings such as workshops, mines, law courts, studies, builder's yards, and hospitals, as well as in the presence of laborers, customers, and workers, as well as in the presence of work that is done well or poorly, expensive or profitable, all contribute to the development of ideas.

These insignificant senses of detail are obtained through the eyes, hands, ears, and even the sense of smell. These senses are involuntarily picked up and silently elaborated, taking shape within the learner and eventually suggesting to him this or that new combination, simplification, economy, improvement.

At least nine out of ten people have squandered time and suffering during telling, significant, even pivotal years of their lives. First among these are the half or two thirds of people who show up for an examination — I mean, those who are turned away; after that, there are still half or two thirds of people — I mean, the overworked — among those who succeed and receive a degree, certificate, or diploma. They have been asked to perform too much, including sitting in a chair or in front of a board for two hours straight on a given day, and being live examples of all human knowledge with regard to a particular set of sciences.

The distinguished psychologist then demonstrates to us how our system differs from the Anglo-Saxons'. They don't have access to our numerous special schools. They base training on object lessons rather than book learning. For instance, training for engineers takes place in a workshop rather than a classroom, enabling each person to develop to the extent that their IQ will allow. If he is unable to advance, he becomes a laborer or a foreman; if his skills allow him to go further, he becomes an engineer. This process is far more democratic and beneficial to society overall than requiring someone to spend their entire career depending on a few-hour exam that they take when they are just.

"The student, who begins at a very young age, goes through his apprenticeship, stage by stage, at the hospital, mine, factory, architect's or lawyer's office, just as done with us a law clerk in his office, or an artist in his studio. He has already had the chance to follow a general and summary course of instruction before beginning a practical journey, in order to have a framework available in which to store the observations he is about to make. In addition, he can typically take advantage of several technical courses during his free time to gradually organize the daily experience he is accumulating.

Regarding the increasing discrepancy between our Latin educational system and the demands of real-world life, the great philosopher comes to the following conclusion: "In the three stages of instruction, childhood, adolescence, and youth, the theoretical and pedagogic preparation by books on the school benches has lengthened out and become overcharged in view of the examination, the degree, the diploma, and the certificate, and solely in this view, and by the worst methods, by the application of an unnatural and anti-social regime, by the excessive postponement of the practical apprenticeship, by our boarding-school system, by artificial training and mechanical cramming, by overwork, without consideration for the adult age and the function.

Have we strayed from the psychology of crowds in the past?

Without a doubt not. It's important to understand how the foundation has been laid if we hope to comprehend the concepts and views that the general public is embracing today and will adopt tomorrow. A nation's youth receive teaching that enables them to learn about the future of their nation. The most pessimistic predictions are justified by the education given to the current generation. Education and instruction play a role in shaping the collective consciousness of a people. As a result, it became imperative to demonstrate how the current system has shaped this thinking and how the majority of indifferent and neutral people have gradually changed.

Chapter II.

The Immediate Factors of the Opinions of Crowds

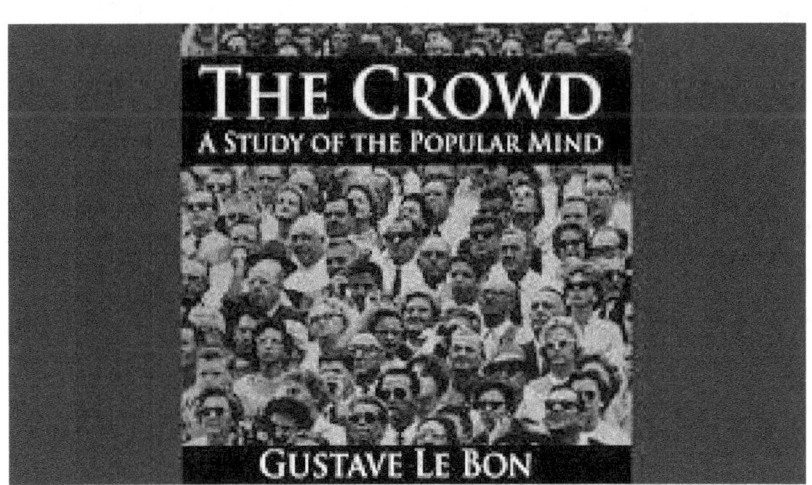

CHAPTER II.

1. Words, pictures, and formulas. Word decay; instances of notable shifts in meaning of frequently used expressions; the enchanted power of words and formulas; the power of words associated with the images they evoke, regardless of their true meaning; these images differ between racial and age groups; the political strategy of renaming things when their previous names had a detrimental effect on the public; disparities in racial perceptions through language; and the definitions of "democracy" in Europe and America.
2. Illusions. Illusions are important because they are the cornerstone of all civilizations and because people are used to accepting them as more important than reality. 3. Background.

We have just looked into the peripheral and preliminary elements that contribute to the unique responsiveness of crowds' minds and enable the development of certain emotions and concepts there. It is now up to us to research the variables that have the potential to act directly. In an upcoming chapter, we will examine how these elements should be implemented to have their maximum impact.

We examined the thoughts, feelings, and reasoning processes of collective bodies in the first section of our study, and it was clear from the information we gained that it would be easy to infer, broadly speaking, how to leave an impact on their minds. We already know what catches people's attention in large groups.

1. Images, Words, and Formulas

We discovered that crowds' imaginations are more receptive to the feelings that visuals evoke. Although these visuals aren't always readily available, they may be conjured up with careful word and formula selection. When handled artistically, they actually hold the enigmatic power that magicians formerly ascribed to them. They incite the most powerful tempests to arise in the minds of multitudes, which they can then calm. All it would take to erect a pyramid considerably higher than the one built by ancient Cheops would be the bones of those who fell prey to the persuasiveness of words and formulae. The pictures that words conjure up are integral to their potency.

Certain words and formulations cannot be defeated by reason or reasoning. In front of large gatherings, they are spoken solemnly, and as soon as they are said, everyone bows their head and every face displays reverence. Many people view them as otherworldly powers or as natural forces. Though they arouse lofty and nebulous thoughts in men's imaginations, it is precisely this ambiguity that envelops them in mystery that heightens their enigmatic potency. These are the enigmatic deities concealed beneath the tabernacle, whom the pious only approach with trepidation and terror.

The pictures conjured up by words are sense-neutral; they differ from person to person and from age to age, but the formulae stay the same.

When a specific language is investigated, it becomes evident that although the words that make up the language change relatively slowly throughout time, the meanings or pictures that these words inspire change constantly.

This is the reason I came to the opinion that it is completely impossible to translate a language, especially one that is dead, in another work. When we try to read a book written in our own language two or three centuries ago, or even when we replace a

Latin, Greek, or Sanscrit term with a French one, what actually happens? We just substitute the concepts and pictures that contemporary life has given us for perfect intelligence.

Again, at a time when the possibility of intellectual liberty was not even suspected and when talking about the gods, the laws, and the city's customs was the only serious crime, what meaning could the word "liberty" have that is even remotely similar to what we associate with it today? For an Athen or Spartan, what could a phrase like "fatherland" mean unless it referred to the religion of Sparta or Athens, not Greece, which was made up of competing towns that were perpetually at war with one another? What significance did the term "fatherland" have for the ancient Gauls, who were easily defeated and split up into competing tribes and races with various languages and religions?

Therefore, words only have ephemeral meanings that vary with age and individual; therefore, in order to use words to influence a crowd, we need to understand the meaning that the crowd currently assigns to them, not the meaning that the words may have in the future for people with different mental constitutions.

Consequently, the first responsibility of a true statesman is to alter the language when large crowds have developed a strong dislike for the images conjured up by certain words as a result of political upheavals or changes in beliefs. This should be done without actually touching the objects themselves, as they are too closely associated with.

Thus, one of the most important roles of statesmen is to rename things that the public cannot stand under popular or, at the very least, indifferent terms. Because of the immense power of words, all that is necessary to make them palatable to large audiences is to label the most repulsive objects with well chosen terminology. Taine correctly points out that the Jacobins were able "to install a despotism worthy of Dahomey, a tribunal similar to that of the Inquisition, and to accomplish human hecatombs akin to those of ancient Mexico" by appealing to liberty and fraternity — words that were quite popular at the time. Like the art of advocates, the art of those in power mostly consists on the science of word choice.

In actuality, they align with quite disparate concepts and perceptions within the Latin and Anglo-Saxon psyche. For the people of Latin America, the term "democracy" primarily refers to the individual's will and initiative being subordinated to the will and initiative of the community as represented by the State. To an increasing extent, the State has the responsibility for overseeing all aspects, including centralization, monopolization, and manufacturing. All political parties, whether they radical, socialist, or monarchist, are in continual appeal to the State. Among the Anglo-Saxons, and particularly in America, this same word "democracy" denotes, on the other hand, the vigorous development of the individual's will and the fullest possible subjection.

1. Illusions

Illusions have always had an impact on crowds, even since the beginning of civilization. More temples, sculptures, and shrines have been erected for illusionists than for any other class of individuals. These powerful sovereign forces are always at the head of every civilization that has progressively grown on our planet, regardless of the religious illusions of the past or the philosophical and social illusions of the present.

CHAPTER II.

Not a single one of our ideas about politics, art, or society is related to the great revolution that rocked all of Europe a century ago, or the temples of Chaldea and Egypt or the religious structures of the Middle Ages.

What would become of humanity's lofty aspirations if all the artistic creations that have been inspired by various faiths were demolished from museums and libraries, and all the works and monuments were toppled in front of churches like flagstones? The purpose of gods, heroes, and poets is to provide mankind with the illusion and hope that they are unable to survive without. It seems that science took up this endeavor over the course of fifty years. However, because science cannot lie, it has become tainted in the hearts that yearn for the ideal and does not dare to make extravagant enough promises."

The last century's thinkers fiercely committed themselves to dispelling the social, political, and religious myths that our ancestors had held.

1. Experience

Experience is essentially the only method that may effectively solidify a truth in the minds of the public and dispel delusions that have become too hazardous. In order to do this, though, a very large-scale and regular repetition of the experience is required. Historical facts that are quoted in order to make a point are meaningless since, generally speaking, the experiences of one generation have no bearing on the generation that follows. Their sole purpose is to demonstrate the degree to which life events must be repeated in order to have any impact or to successfully challenge a false belief that has become deeply ingrained in the minds.

The French Revolution was the largest of these attempts. It was required to murder several million people and severely disrupt Europe for twenty years in order to discover that a society cannot be completely transformed in line with the principles of pure reason. Two disastrous events had to occur in fifty years to demonstrate to us empirically that tyrants cost the countries that support them dearly, yet despite their clarity, they don't appear to have been compelling enough. However, the first required an invasion and three million soldiers, while the second resulted in territory loss and the need for permanent armies.

1. Reason

If it weren't essential to highlight reason's detrimental impact, every mention of reason in the list of elements that have the power to sway mob opinion may be skipped.

As demonstrated previously, crowds are unaffected by reason and are only able to understand crude correlations between concepts. Speakers who have the ability to leave an effect on individuals constantly appeal to their emotions rather than their logic. In crowds, the laws of reasoning are inapplicable.16 In order to instill conviction in audiences, one must first fully understand the feelings that motivate them, then act as though you share these feelings, and last try to change them by making calls to,

Understanding the complete helplessness of reason in the face of emotion is possible without even going as low as primordial creatures. Let us just recall how persistent religious beliefs have been, defying even the most basic reasoning, for generations. The brightest minds on earth have submitted to their laws for almost two millennia; their validity must be challenged in the present period. There were many bright persons during the Middle Ages and the Renaissance, but not one of them arrived to this level by appreciating the ridiculous aspects of his beliefs or by fostering even the slightest doubt about the evils of the devil or the necessity.

Is it regrettable that reason never leads a crowd? We wouldn't risk confirming it. Without a doubt, human reason could not have inspired mankind to pursue civilization with the fervor and resilience that its illusions have. These delusions, which are the result of the unconscious forces that guide us, were undoubtedly required. All races possess inherent in their mental structure the rules governing their fate, and it is these laws that they may follow without hesitation, even when their inclinations seem the most irrational. Sometimes it appears that mysterious powers, similar to those that push an acorn to become an oak, control whole nations.

Chapter III.

The Leaders of Crowds and Their Means of Persuasion

CHAPTER III.

1. The crowd leaders. All creatures who form a crowd have an innate need to follow a leader. This is known as the psychology of crowd leaders. Only they possess the ability to organize and instill trust in their followers. The leaders may also be violently tyrannical. The leaders are classified according to the role that the will plays. 2. The leaders' methods of operation. Repetition, affirmation, and contagion — Each of these components — The potential for contagion to go from lower to higher social strata in a society — A popular belief quickly becomes a common

opinion. 3. Prestige. Definition of prestige and categorization of its many forms; Personal and acquired prestige; Examples; Methods by which prestige is lost.

We now understand the mental makeup of crowds and the kind of motivations that might leave an effect on their minds. It is yet up to examine how and by whom these incentives may be put into meaningful practical use.

1. **The Leaders of Crowds.**

Upon the gathering of a specific quantity of organisms, whether they humans or animals, they automatically subordinate themselves to a leader.

The leader of a human crowd is typically only an organizer or provocateur, but even so, he has a significant influence. His will serves as the center around which the general public's viewpoints are assembled and given shape. He is the initial step in organizing diverse groups of people and prepares the path for them to organize into sects while leading them in the meantime. A mob is a subservient herd incapable of functioning on its own without a leader.

Most of the time, the leader was once one of the led. He has become an advocate of the notion, having been hypnotized by it himself. He has become so enmeshed in it that everything outside of it disappears and he perceives every opposing viewpoint as a mistake or superstition. One such instance is Robespierre, who was captivated by Rousseau's intellectual concepts and used the Inquisition's techniques to spread them.

More often than not, the leaders we discuss are men of action rather than intellectuals. They could never have been endowed with acute foresight, as this trait usually breeds uncertainty and passivity.

Although there has never been a dearth of leaders in a nation, none of them have ever been driven by the fervent beliefs characteristic of apostles. These leaders frequently use clever language to persuade others while just looking out for themselves and appealing to their primal desires. Even while they can exert a lot of power in this way, it is always fleeting. The men of the French Revolution, the Luthers, the Savonarolas, Peter the Hermits, and other men with strong views who have captivated large crowds have only used their interest after initially being enthralled with a faith. They can then invoke that powerful energy known as faith in their colleagues' souls, which makes a man.

The job of great crowd leaders has always been to inspire faith, whether it religious, political, or social; faith in a work, in a person, or in a concept. For this reason, their power is always extremely strong. Faith has always been one of the most powerful tools available to humanity, and the gospel properly claims that it has the ability to move mountains. Giving a guy trust is like giving him 10 times more power. The biggest historical events have been influenced by obscurant believers whose only advantage has been their religion. It is not with the support of the educated, philosophers, or even skeptics that have.

However, in the aforementioned situations, we are dealing with exceptional leaders who are so rare that history can readily account for them. They are the pinnacle of an unbroken chain that starts with these strongmen and ends with the laborer who, in the smoky atmosphere of a pub, gradually enthralls his companions by repeatedly beating into their ears a few predetermined phrases, the meaning of which he hardly understands but whose application, in his opinion, must undoubtedly result in the fulfillment of all hopes and dreams.

In all social circles, from the top to the bottom, a man quickly succumbs to the sway of a leader the moment he stops feeling alone.

Crowd leaders exercise an extremely tyrannical power, and gaining a following really depends on them maintaining this tyranny. It has frequently been observed how effortlessly they extract obedience from the most unruly segment of the working classes, while having no way of justifying their power. They also set the salary and work hours, as well as the start and finish times of strikes, which they choose.

These days, these leaders and agitators have a tendency to usurp the position of public authorities in proportion to how much the latter let themselves to be questioned and stripped of their authority. Because of these new lords' despotism, the masses submit to them.

There are two distinct types of these agitators and ringleaders. There are two types of men: those who are very motivated and have strong willpower occasionally, and those who are considerably less common than the ones who came before them and whose willpower is constant. The first three are bold, aggressive, and daring. They are particularly helpful in leading an unexpected violent endeavor, rallying the populace despite peril, and turning guys who were only recruits yesterday into heroes. Such guys like Ney and Murat existed throughout the First Empire, and in our own day, one such man was Garibaldi, an enthusiastic but untalented explorer who managed to get with a small group of men.

The man who successfully divided the Eastern and Western

worlds is the most recent example of what can be achieved by a strong and persistent will. For three millennia, the greatest sovereigns had tried in vain to accomplish the same job. He eventually failed in a similar endeavor, but by then old age had set in, when everything, including willpower, crumbles.

To demonstrate the potential achieved via sheer determination, all that has to be done is provide a detailed account of the challenges faced during the Suez Canal's construction. Dr. Cazalis, one of the eyewitnesses, has succinctly summarized the complete.

2. The Means of Action of the Leaders: Affirmation, Repetition, Contagion

The crowd must be moved by quick suggestion, of which example has the greatest impact, in order to incite it to commit an act of any kind, such as plundering a palace or dying in defense of a stronghold or barricade, for a brief period of time. However, in order to achieve this goal, the audience must have been pre-prepared by specific conditions and, most importantly, the person wishing to work on it must have the attribute that will be further examined, which I refer to as prestige.

On the other hand, when it is suggested that a crowd's minds be filled with concepts and opinions — with contemporary social theories,

A straightforward, unadulterated affirmation, devoid of any logic or evidence, is one of the most reliable ways to get a concept into the minds of large numbers of people. An statement has greater weight the more conciser it is, the more devoid of any semblance of evidence and demonstration. Throughout history, legal rules and religious texts have consistently relied on straightforward affirmation. Affirmation is valuable to both commercial persons driving product sales through advertising and statesmen called upon to support a political cause. However, until affirmation is consistently given in as many same phrases as possible, it has no meaningful impact.

When the power repetition has over even the most informed brains is considered, its impact over crowds becomes understandable. This power stems from the repeated statement's long-term embedding in the deepest parts of our unconscious selves, where our actions' motivations are shaped. After a while, we stop remembering who originally said the repeated claim, and we come to believe it. The incredible influence of ads is to blame for this situation. When we After reading hundreds or thousands of times that X's chocolate is the greatest, we envision hearing this from several sources and come to the conclusion that this.

When the power repetition has over even the most informed brains is considered, its impact over crowds becomes understandable. This power stems from the repeated statement's long-term embedding in the deepest parts of our unconscious selves, where our actions' motivations are shaped. After a while, we stop remembering who originally said the repeated claim, and we come to believe it. The incredible influence of ads is to blame for this situation. When we

What is known as a current of opinion forms and the potent mechanism of contagion steps in when an affirmation has been sufficiently repeated and there is unanimity in this repetition — as has happened in the case of certain well-known financial undertakings rich enough to purchase every assistance. Crowds of ideas, sentiments, emotions, and beliefs have an infectious capacity comparable to that of germs. Given that it occurs even in groups of animals, this phenomena is quite normal. If one horse in a barn starts biting his manger, the other horses will follow suit. When fear attacks a few sheep, it quickly spreads to the entire herd.

When the power repetition has over even the most informed brains is considered, its impact over crowds becomes understandable. This power stems from the repeated statement's long-term embedding in the deepest parts of our unconscious selves, where our actions' motivations are shaped. After a while, we stop remembering who originally said the repeated claim, and we come to believe it. The incredible influence of ads is to blame for this situation. When we

It is not necessary for people to be in the same place at the same time in order for them to contract a disease. The phenomenon of contagion may be observed at a distance due to circumstances that imbue each person with a unique pattern and the traits unique to a group. This is particularly the case when those distant factors — about which I have conducted a study — have primed men's thoughts to be affected in issue. The revolutionary movement of 1848, which began in Paris and quickly swept across much of Europe and several thrones, serves as an illustration of this.

In actuality, imitation — which is given a lot of credit in social phenomena — is really a byproduct of transmission. After demonstrating its.

When the power repetition has over even the most informed brains is considered, its impact over crowds becomes understandable. This power stems from the repeated statement's long-term embedding in the deepest parts of our unconscious selves, where our actions' motivations are shaped. After a while, we stop remembering who originally said the repeated claim, and we come to believe it. The incredible influence of ads is to blame for this situation. When we

In the long run, the dual actions of the past and reciprocal imitation make all men of the same country and era so alike that, even in the case of those who would seem destined to elude this double influence, like philosophers, learned men, and men of letters, their style and thought have a family air that makes it easy to recognize the age to which they belong. It's not essential to have a lengthy conversation with someone in order to fully understand what they read, what they do for a living, and their environment."17

Because contagion has so great power, people are forced to adopt particular viewpoints and emotional patterns.

When the power repetition has over even the most informed brains is considered, its impact over crowds becomes understandable. This power stems from the repeated statement's long-term embedding in the deepest parts of our unconscious selves, where our actions' motivations are shaped. After a while, we stop remembering who originally said the repeated claim, and we come to believe it. The incredible influence of ads is to blame for this situation. When we

It should be emphasized that in situations similar to the ones I just mentioned, the popular classes have been affected by the virus, which has then spread to the upper social groups. This is what we observe happening right now in regards to the socialist ideas that individuals who will ultimately become their first victims are starting to adopt. The force of contagion is so strong that it even subdues sentiments of personal interest. This explains why, despite the seeming irrationality of the winning viewpoint, any idea that the people adopts always manages to firmly establish itself among the highest social strata.

1. Prestige

When the power repetition has over even the most informed brains is considered, its impact over crowds becomes understandable. This power stems from the repeated statement's long-term embedding in the deepest parts of our unconscious selves, where our actions' motivations are shaped. After a while, we stop remembering who originally said the repeated claim, and we come to believe it. The incredible influence of ads is to blame for this situation. When we

Ideas that spread via confirmation, reiteration, and virality are endowed with great power because they gradually come to possess the enigmatic quality known as reputation. Any dominant force in history, be it ideas or people, has mostly maintained its dominance by the unstoppable force embodied in the term "prestige." Although everyone understands the meaning of the phrase, there are too many variations in its use for it to be simply defined. A person's prestige may evoke feelings of dread or adoration. It can exist without these feelings, yet sometimes they serve as its foundation.

When the power repetition has over even the most informed brains is considered, its impact over crowds becomes understandable. This power stems from the repeated statement's long-term embedding in the deepest parts of our unconscious selves, where our actions' motivations are shaped. After a while, we stop remembering who originally said the repeated claim, and we come to believe it. The incredible influence of ads is to blame for this situation. When we

In actuality, prestige is a kind of mental dominance that

someone, something, or an idea exercises over us. Our ability to think critically is completely paralyzed by this dominance, which instills awe and reverence in our hearts. Like other emotions, the one evoked is incomprehensible, but it seems to be similar to the curiosity that a person who is magnetized is drawn to. The foundation of all authority is prestige. There has never been a reigning god, king, or woman without it.

Two main categories may be used to classify the different types of prestige: acquired prestige and personal prestige. The prestige that comes from name, wealth, and reputation is known as acquired prestige. It might not rely on one's social standing.

When the power repetition has over even the most informed brains is considered, its impact over crowds becomes understandable. This power stems from the repeated statement's long-term embedding in the deepest parts of our unconscious selves, where our actions' motivations are shaped. After a while, we stop remembering who originally said the repeated claim, and we come to believe it. The incredible influence of ads is to blame for this situation. When we

The prestige I just mentioned is exerted by individuals; it may also be exercised by ideas, literary and artistic works, and other things. The latter form of prestige typically stems from a series of cumulative repeats. History — literary and artistic history in particular — is nothing more than the reiteration of the same conclusions that no one bothers to check, so everyone just repeats what they were taught in school until things start to take on names and characteristics that no one would dare to touch. Reading Homer is undoubtedly quite boring for readers in the present day, but who would dare say that? The Parthenon is a miserable ruin that lacks any attraction in the modern day, however it is.

CHAPTER III.

When the power repetition has over even the most informed brains is considered, its impact over crowds becomes understandable. This power stems from the repeated statement's long-term embedding in the deepest parts of our unconscious selves, where our actions' motivations are shaped. After a while, we stop remembering who originally said the repeated claim, and we come to believe it. The incredible influence of ads is to blame for this situation. When we

Let me now discuss personal prestige. Its nature differs greatly from that of acquired or fake status, which is what I was just talking about. It is a capacity that is apart from all titles and powers, held by a select few people who, while being social equals and devoid of any conventional methods of dominance, are able to exert a really magnetic interest on others around them. They compel everyone around them to share their opinions and feelings, and they are obeyed in the same way that an animal that might easily eat him tames wild monsters.

This type of status has been held by famous crowd leaders including Buddha, Jesus, Mahomet, Joan of Arc, and Napoleon.

When the power repetition has over even the most informed brains is considered, its impact over crowds becomes understandable. This power stems from the repeated statement's long-term embedding in the deepest parts of our unconscious selves, where our actions' motivations are shaped. After a while, we stop remembering who originally said the repeated claim, and we come to believe it. The incredible influence of ads is to blame for this situation. When we

The great figures I just mentioned had the ability to fascinate people long before they rose to prominence, and they could not have done so without it. For example, it is clear that Napoleon, even at the height of his glory, had a great deal of prestige just by virtue of his position of authority, but this prestige was partially previously bestowed upon him while he was absolutely unknown and powerless. As an insignificant general, he was appointed to lead the army of Italy due to his protection, and he found himself surrounded by tough generals who planned to greet the youthful interloper sent by the Directory with hostility. Without the use of lectures, right from the start, at the initial interview,

When the power repetition has over even the most informed brains is considered, its impact over crowds becomes understandable. This power stems from the repeated statement's long-term embedding in the deepest parts of our unconscious selves, where our actions' motivations are shaped. After a while, we stop remembering who originally said the repeated claim, and we come to believe it. The incredible influence of ads is to blame for this situation. When we

grow to be a great man, his stature rising in direct proportion to his radiance, and in the eyes of his devotees, he attained the status of a deity. "That devil of a man exercises a fascination on me that I cannot explain even to myself, and in such a degree that, though I fear neither God nor devil, when I am in his presence I am ready to tremble like a child, and he could make me go through the eye of a needle," General Vandamme, a rough, typical soldier of the Revolution, even more brutal and energetic than Augereau, said of him to Marshal d'Arnano in 1815.

When the power repetition has over even the most informed brains is considered, its impact over crowds becomes understandable. This power stems from the repeated statement's long-term embedding in the deepest parts of our unconscious selves, where our actions' motivations are shaped. After a while, we stop remembering who originally said the repeated claim, and we come to believe it. The incredible influence of ads is to

CHAPTER III.

blame for this situation. When we

To comprehend that marvelous return from the Isle of Elba and that lightning-like conquest of France by an isolated man facing all the organized forces of a great country that might have been thought to be tired of his tyranny, one must keep in mind the astounding power exerted by this order's fascination. All he needed to do was glance at the generals who had been assigned to apprehend him and had pledged to carry out their task. They all turned in their forms without talking.

"Napoleon," the English General Wolseley recalls, "arrives in France nearly alone, a fugitive from the little island of Elba which was his kingdom, and succeeds in a few weeks, without violence, in upending all organized power in France under its rightful.

When the power repetition has over even the most informed brains is considered, its impact over crowds becomes understandable. This power stems from the repeated statement's long-term embedding in the deepest parts of our unconscious selves, where our actions' motivations are shaped. After a while, we stop remembering who originally said the repeated claim, and we come to believe it. The incredible influence of ads is to blame for this situation.

When the power repetition has over even the most informed brains is considered, its impact over crowds becomes understandable. This power stems from the repeated statement's long-term embedding in the deepest parts of our unconscious selves, where our actions' motivations are shaped. After a while, we stop remembering who originally said the repeated claim, and we come to believe it. The incredible influence of ads is to blame for this situation. When we

He no longer saw barriers and planned to start Suez over in

Panama after "having vanquished whatever there is to vanquish, men and things, marshes, rocks, and sandy wastes." He started over using the same techniques as before, but he was older now, and moreover, if a faith is too high, it won't move mountains. The hero's glistening aureole of glory was shattered by the devastation that followed when the mountains refused to yield. His life serves as an example of how status can both increase and decrease. He once rivaled the greatest heroes in history in terms of brilliance, but the judges in his nation demoted him to the lowest class of criminals.

When the power repetition has over even the most informed brains is considered, its impact over crowds becomes understandable. This power stems from the repeated statement's long-term embedding in the deepest parts of our unconscious selves, where our actions' motivations are shaped. After a while, we stop remembering who originally said the repeated claim, and we come to believe it. The incredible influence of ads is to blame for this situation. When we

All the many types of prestige that come from the various disciplines that make up a civilization — the sciences, the arts, literature, and so on — would find a home between the extreme boundaries of this series, and it would become clear that prestige is the essential component of persuasion. Whether they realize it or not, the person, concept, or object that is seen as important is quickly copied as a result of contagion, which compels a whole generation to adopt particular ways of thinking and feeling. Furthermore, this imitation is usually unconscious, which explains why it is flawless. The contemporary artists who emulate the muted hues and rigid demeanors of certain Primitives are seldom cognizant of the origin of their inspiration. They have faith in their own genuineness,

CHAPTER III.

When the power repetition has over even the most informed brains is considered, its impact over crowds becomes understandable. This power stems from the repeated statement's long-term embedding in the deepest parts of our unconscious selves, where our actions' motivations are shaped. After a while, we stop remembering who originally said the repeated claim, and we come to believe it. The incredible influence of ads is to blame for this situation. When we

From what came before, it is clear that a variety of reasons might have contributed to the development of reputation, with achievement consistently ranking among the most crucial. Every successful person and every concept that gains acceptance automatically stops being questioned. The fact that the absence of one nearly invariably coincides with the disappearance of the other is evidence that success is one of the main stepping stones to status. The hero that the audience applauded yesterday is offended if failure has surpassed him today. In fact, the response will be more forceful given the high level of reputation.

9

Chapter IV.

Limitations of the Variability of the Beliefs and Opinions of Crowds

CHAPTER IV.

1. Set beliefs. Certain broad ideas are unchangeable; they influence the development of civilizations; they are difficult to eradicate; in certain cases, intolerance is a virtue in a people; and their logical ridiculousness cannot stop a belief from spreading. 2. The malleable views of masses. The tremendous mobility of perspectives that are not based on shared beliefs — Variations in concepts and viewpoints in less than a century — The actual boundaries of these variations — The issues that the variation affects — Opinions these days are more malleable due to the tremendous spread of the daily press and the current decline in the advancement of popular ideas. This explains why the majority of issues tend to elicit apathy from crowds. Governments are no longer able to shape public opinion as they once did.

1. Fixed Beliefs

The psychological and physical traits of living things are closely linked. Certain invariable or slightly variable components are present in certain anatomical traits, and their change requires a hiatus in geological periods. Beside these unalterable, fixed properties are others that are incredibly variable. These may be readily altered by a skilled breeder or horticulture, sometimes to the point where the basic traits are hidden from an unobservant observer.

When it comes to moral qualities, the similar pattern is seen.

There will be movable and variable components of a race in addition to the unchangeable psychological components. Because of this, while examining a people's views and opinions, the presence is always seen.

Crowd opinions and beliefs may therefore be classified into two quite different kinds. On the one hand, we have deeply ingrained ideas that can last for several centuries and serve as the foundation for a whole civilization.

Examples of such ideologies from the past include feudalism, Christianity, and protestantism; examples from the present include the nationalist ideal and modern democratic and social concepts. Second, there are the ephemeral, shifting viewpoints that are typically the product of broad assumptions that manifest in every era. Theories that influence literature and the arts, such as those that gave rise to romanticism, naturalism, mysticism, and so forth, are prime examples of this.

It is quite easy to ingrain a fleeting notion in the minds of masses, but it is very difficult to establish a conviction that will stick. Nevertheless, once a belief of this latter sort is formed, it is similarly difficult to displace it. Usually, only via bloody revolutions can it be altered. Only until the belief has virtually completely lost its power over men's minds can even revolutions succeed. In that scenario, revolutions help to finally remove things that were on the verge of being abandoned but were held back by habit. In actuality, a belief's demise marks the start of a revolution.

It is easy to identify the exact time when a great conviction is

CHAPTER IV.

doomed; it is the moment when its.

However, even when a belief is profoundly challenged, the institutions it gave rise to endure and eventually fade away. Ultimately, everything that depended on the belief eventually comes to an end when it has entirely lost its power. Until now, no country has been able to alter its ideas without also being forced to completely overhaul its whole civilization. The country keeps going through this change process until it has come to terms with and adopted a new national belief: up to this point, it is inevitably in a state of anarchy. The fundamental cornerstones of civilizations are universal beliefs, which set the direction of intellectual thought. They are the only ones who can arouse faith and a sense of obligation.

Countries have always recognized the need of forming broad ideas and have an innate understanding that the loss of these beliefs would indicate the beginning of the end for their own development. Rome was destined to perish because of the Romans' fervent worship, which gave them the illusion that they were the lords of the universe. Regarding the barbarians that destroyed Roman civilization, they only achieved some degree of unity and moved out of chaos once they came to have some widely held ideas.It is obvious that nations have consistently shown intolerance in the defense of their beliefs. This intolerance, which is susceptible to philosophical critique, is a representation.

Establishing a widespread belief is quite tough, but once it is well ingrained, its strength is unstoppable for a very long time, and regardless of how erroneous it may be philosophically, it impresses itself upon the most brilliant mind. For almost 150 years, the European peoples have been considered infallible due to their religious tales, which upon closer inspection are just as savage as those of Moloch. For many years, people were unaware of the terrifying ridiculousness of the story of a God torturing his son in order to exact retribution on him for the disobedience of one of his animals. Prominent intellectuals like Galileo, Newton, and Leibnitz never imagined for a second that the veracity of such beliefs might be put into question.

Although temporary auxiliary thoughts may emerge from the core belief, they will always have the imprint of the original belief.

A limited number of religious ideas that have left their imprint on the least significant aspects of these civilizations and allowed for their rapid detection have led to the development of three distinct civilizations: the Egyptian civilization, the Middle Ages European civilization, and the Arab Mussulman civilization.

Because of prevailing ideas, men of all ages are therefore enmeshed in a web of habits, attitudes, and traditions that make them all identical and from which they are unable to free themselves. Men are mostly directed in their behavior by their beliefs and the norms that follow from those beliefs.

The intellectual nonsense that frequently characterizes popular ideas has never prevented them from succeeding. It's true that the success of these ideas would appear unlikely unless they provided some sort of enigmatic absurdity. Therefore, the obvious flaws in modern socialist doctrine won't stop them from becoming popular among the public. Their actual inferiority to all religious ideas stems exclusively from the realization that no one could really challenge the latter's ideal of happiness, which could only be realized in a future life. The socialist ideal of happiness is meant to be realized on earth, but as soon as the first steps are taken to make that happen, the folly of its promises will immediately become apparent.

CHAPTER IV.

2. The Changeable Opinions of Crowds

Overlying the foundation of solid beliefs—the strength of which we have just seen—is an overabundance of constantly emerging and vanishing views, ideas, and thoughts. A few of them are fleeting, and the most significant ones hardly last a generation. As we have already mentioned, racial factors are constantly at play when it comes to the shifts in beliefs of this kind, and they are sometimes far more superficial than genuine. Examining the French political system, for example, we demonstrated that parties that appear to be completely different—royalists, radicals, imperialists, socialists, and so forth—have an ideal that is exactly the same, and that this ideal is only based on the mental makeup of the French people because an entirely different ideal can be found.

For illustration, let's look at a very brief segment of French history: the thirty-year span, or generation, from 1790 to 1820. Throughout, we witness the mob go from being initially monarchical to being extremely revolutionary, imperialist, and back to being monarchical. Religion tends to move in the same direction over time: from Catholicism to atheism, then to deism, and finally back to the most extreme versions of Catholicism. These shifts affect not just the populace but also the people in charge of them. We watch in dismay as the well-known Convention participants—men who were sworn foes of monarchs and who would have no gods or masters—become the meek servants.

Even faster sequential evolutions of opinion may be seen in philosophy, art, and literature. In turn, naturalism, mysticism, romanticism, and so forth emerge and fade. The writer and artist who were praised the day before are regarded with extreme disdain the next day.

But what do we discover when we examine all these recent changes in appearance? Any individual who disagrees with the prevailing ideas and emotions of the race is fleeting, and the stream quickly turns back toward its original direction. Opinions that are not based on any prevailing racial idea or attitude, and as a result are unstable, are subject to random fluctuations or, if desired, shifts in the external environment.

First, the old ideas are no longer able to impact the fleeting attitudes of the time the way they once did since they are losing ground on a growing scale. As common ideas erode, a crop of random viewpoints with no apparent past or future emerge.

The second reason is that, as crowd power grows and becomes less and less counterbalanced, the high mobility of ideas — which has been identified as a characteristic of crowds — can materialize without restriction.

The newspaper press's recent growth, which has allowed for the constant presentation of the most opposing viewpoints before readers, is the final and third factor.

Thus, the consensus of the masses increasingly tends to be the governing principle in politics. These days, it even goes so far as to impose partnerships, as the Franco-Russian alliance, which is the only result of a public movement, has demonstrated recently. Popes, kings, and emperors agreeing to be interviewed in order to submit their opinions on a particular topic to the opinion of the masses is an odd sign of the modern day. It used to be true to assert that politics had nothing to do with feeling. Is the same true now, when politics are more affected by the whims of volatile masses that are immune to reason and solely susceptible to emotion?

The primary focus of governments and the press these days is closely monitoring the evolution of public opinion. Nothing is more mobile and changeable than the thought of crowds, and nothing is more frequent than witnessing them execute today what they cheered yesterday. Therefore, the effect produced by an event, a legislative proposal, or a speech is exactly what they need to know.

The ultimate result of this complete lack of any kind of opinion direction and the simultaneous dismantling of general beliefs has been an extreme divergence of convictions of every order and a growing apathy on the part of crowds to everything that does not directly affect their immediate interests.

Due to debate and study, opinions these days are becoming less and less respected; their unique qualities are quickly eroding, and only a select handful remain that may pique our curiosity. The modern man is becoming an increasingly easy target for apathy.

Opinions are generally worn thin, therefore it's hardly worth lamenting too much. It is indisputable that it is a sign of decadence among a population. It is undeniable that individuals with extraordinary, nearly supernatural insight, apostles, crowd leaders, or simply people with sincere, strong convictions, wield far more power than those who reject, criticize, or show no interest in anything. However, it should not be overlooked that, considering the current level of power.

Book III.

The Classification and Description of the Different Kinds of Crowds

CHAPTER IV.

10

Chapter I.

The Classification of Crowds

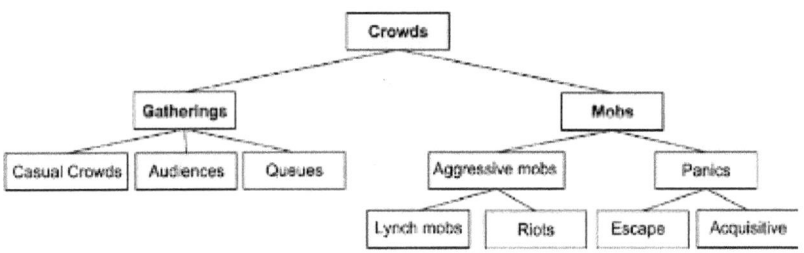

CHAPTER I.

The classification of crowds and their main divisions. 1. Diverse assemblages. Various kinds of them; the effect of race; the crowd's spirit is feeble in proportion to the race's strength; the race's spirit symbolizes the civilized state, while the crowd's spirit depicts the barbaric condition. 2. Even groups of people. Their many forms — classes, castes, and sects.

In this paper, we have outlined the general traits shared by psychological crowds. It is still necessary to identify the specific traits that go along with the general order in the various kinds of communities when they become a crowd due to the right stimulating factors. Firstly, we will briefly present a categorization system for crowds.

The basic many will serve as our beginning point. When people of different ethnicities make up the multitude, it takes on its most deplorable form. In this instance, the chief's will, which is generally accepted, is the sole thing uniting them. One may mention the many different kinds of barbarians who overran the Roman Empire over a number of centuries.

These two types of multitudes have the potential to become organized or psychological crowds under some of the circumstances this book examines. These organized groups will be divided into the following sections: —

A. Diverse assemblages.

1. Unidentified groups of people, such those on the street.

2. Non-anonymous crowds in settings like parliamentary assemblies and juries.

B. Even groups of people.

1. Sects (religious, political, and so on).

2. Castes (such as the working caste, religious caste, military caste, and so on).

3. Classes (peasant, middle, and other classes).

We will briefly highlight the traits that set these various population types different.

1. Heterogeneous Crowds

The features of these collectivities have been examined in this volume. They are made up of people with many kinds of characteristics, occupations, and IQ levels.

We now know that men's collective psychology differs fundamentally from their individual psychology just by virtue of being members of a crowd involved in action, and that this difference has an impact on men's intellect. As we've shown, intelligence has little effect on societies; instead, unconscious feelings are the only thing that shape them.

Racial diversity is a basic characteristic that makes it possible to distinguish between the different diverse crowds fairly well. We have previously discussed race's role several times and demonstrated that it is the most potent element capable.

When, as is rarely the case, people of different nationalities come together in one group and in relatively equal numbers, even if their shared interests are what initially sparked the gathering, the stark differences in men's inherited mental constitutions' ways of feeling and thinking immediately come into focus. The socialists' attempts to bring together representatives of working-class people from many nations in large congresses have always resulted in the most severe conflict. No matter how radical or conservative they may seem, a Latino mob will always look to the government to step in and fulfill their demands. It may always be identified by its clear inclination toward centralization and its more or less obvious.

Therefore, a crowd's dispositions are greatly influenced by the genius of the race. The strong underlying drive is what restricts its humor shifts. The idea that the weaker aspects of crowds are less prominent in proportion to the strength of the race should be regarded as a fundamental law. The barbarian state, or a return to it, is equated with the crowd state and the dominance of crowds. Through the development of a strong sense of collective identity, the race gradually breaks away from the unthinking influence of large groups and transcends the state of barbarians. The sole significant categorization of diverse groups, other from the one predicated on.

2. Homogeneous Crowds

The following groups are homogeneous: 1. Sects; 2. Castes; 3. Classes.

The formation of a sect is the initial stage in the organization of homogenous masses. With their shared views serving as the unifying factor, members of a sect might differ significantly in terms of their education, careers, and social class. Political and religious groups are two examples of this.

The greatest level of organization to which the populace is prone is represented by the caste. The caste is made up of people who share the same profession and, therefore, are similarly educated and of a similar social status, whereas the sect is made up of people with very different occupations, levels of education, and social backgrounds who are only connected by the beliefs they share.

11

Chapter II.

Crowds Termed Criminal Crowds

CHAPTER II.

The term "criminal crowds" refers to groups of people who may be legally complicit but not psychologically — The complete unawareness of crowd behavior — Different instances — The writers of the September atrocities' psychological state — Their morals, their wrath, their sensibility, and their logic.

It appears impossible to classify crowds as criminal in any event since, following a time of enthusiasm, they descend into a completely automatic and unconscious condition where they are directed by suggestion. I only hold onto this incorrect qualifier because subsequent psychological research has undoubtedly made it more popular. If viewed in isolation, some crowd behaviors are undoubtedly illegal, but in that scenario, they are illegal in the same sense as when a tiger eats a hindoo after letting its offspring pummel him for entertainment.

The typical motivation for crimes committed by crowds is a strong suggestion, and those who participate in these crimes later believe that their actions were compliant.

One such example would be the assassination of M. de Launay, the governor of the Bastille. The governor was hit from all sides once the stronghold was taken, and he was besieged by a fervent mob.

There were suggestions to hang him, chop off his head, and fasten him to a horse's tail. He kicked one of the people there by mistake as he was fumbling. A suggestion was made, and the people cheered instantly, suggesting that the person who had been kicked should sever the governor's throat. "The person in issue, an unemployed chef, believes that since this is the standard practice, his main motivation for visiting the Bastille was idle curiosity about what was happening.

The general traits we have observed in all crowds — openness to persuasion, credulity, mobility, amplification of positive or negative emotions, display of specific morals, etc. — are also present in criminal crowds.

All of these traits may be found in the throng that carried out the September atrocities, which has left the worst memories in French history behind. Actually, it has a lot in common with the group who carried out the Saint Bartholomew atrocities. I have taken the details from M. Taine's narrative, which was based on sources from the same era. Who specifically issued the order or suggested massacring inmates in order to empty the jails is unknown.

The killers comprised a group of around three hundred individuals, exhibiting a typical diverse crowd. Apart from a few of well-paid thugs, the majority of its members were store owners and craftspeople from various industries, including masons, bootmakers, locksmiths, hair stylists, clerks, messengers, and so on. As was the cook mentioned before, they are completely persuaded that they are carrying out a patriotic duty as a result of the proposal they have received. They hold two positions simultaneously — judges and executioners — but they never think of themselves as criminals.

Being acutely aware of the gravity of their responsibility, they start by setting up a kind of tribunal. In connection with this action, the cleverness of the masses and their crude.

"They possess the immediate intuition and broad compassion of the Parisian working man. After discovering that the inmates had gone without water for 26 hours, one of the federates at the Abbaye was determined to execute the guard and would have succeeded if not for the inmates' pleading. Everyone, including the guards and the slaughterers, hugs and cheers wildly when a prisoner is found not guilty (by the makeshift trial), and then the massive carnage resumes. As it advances, a delightful joy never goes away. Around the bodies, there is music and dancing, and chairs are set up "for the ladies," who are happy to watch nobles be killed.

Crowds constantly exhibit such primitive kinds of thinking, which are evident in all of their actions. Therefore, following the massacre of the 1,200–1,500 enemies of the country, someone remarks — and his idea is immediately accepted — that the other prisons — those housing elderly vagrants, young inmates, and beggars — actually house worthless mouths, and it would be wise to remove them for that reason. A lady named Delarue, for example, the widow of a poisoner, should undoubtedly be among them as an enemy of the people: "She must be enraged at being imprisoned; if she could, she would set fire to Paris: she must have said so, she has said so."

The Commune of 1871's history provides a number of facts that are similar to those mentioned earlier. We're going to see a lot more of this kind of thing because of the increasing power of crowds and the authorities' constant surrenders to them.

Chapter III.

Criminal Juries

juries for crimesGenerally speaking, statistics indicate that juries' decisions are made regardless of the makeup of the jury. The ways in which an impression can be made on juries; the argument's style and impact; the strategies used by renowned attorneys to persuade juries; the types of crimes for which juries are either lenient or harsh; the purpose of the jury as an institution; and the risk that would arise from judges taking its place.

I will just look at the most significant kind of jury here, which is the Court of Assize jury. I am not able to study every kind of jury here. These jurors provide a great illustration of a diverse, non-anonymous population. They exhibit suggestibility and a limited ability for reasoning, are susceptible to the influence of crowd leaders, and are primarily motivated by unconscious feelings. Throughout this inquiry, we will see a few fascinating instances of mistakes that people who are not familiar with crowd psychology may make.

First of all, juries provide us with an excellent illustration of the insignificance of the mental state of the various components.

"Today, in actuality, the choice of jurymen rests with the local council members, who rank candidates and remove others based on the political and electoral agendas that naturally arise in their circumstances....

Those in commerce, albeit of lesser prominence than in the past, and workers from certain administrative branches make up the bulk of the jurors selected.... The jury's decisions have stayed the same, despite the fact that both professions and viewpoints were meaningless once the job of judge was taken, many jury members possessing the ardor of novices, and even well-meaning individuals being similarly oriented in lowly circumstances."

CHAPTER III.

It is important to keep in mind the findings of the just-cited chapter rather than the inadequate explanations. It is not necessary to be very shocked by this deficiency because, generally speaking, both attorneys and magistrates appear to be unaware of the psychology of crowds and, by extension, jurors. I find evidence for this claim in the fact that the author just cited. He notes that in the case of every intelligence subject on the list, Lachaud, one of the most renowned attorneys practicing in the Court of Assize, routinely exercised his privilege to object to a jury. However, experience — and experience alone — has shown us that these objections are completely pointless.

Although these crimes are the most hazardous for society, juries show no sympathy for crimes in which the perpetrator seems to be the victim; in contrast, they are quite forgiving when it comes to legal transgressions motivated by emotion. They are rarely harsh on girl-mothers who commit infanticide or harsh on the young woman who lashes out at the man who has wooed and abandoned her because they have an innate sense that such crimes pose little threat to society[24] and that, in a nation where the law does not shield abandoned girls, the crime of the girl taking revenge on her attacker is actually more beneficial than detrimental because it deters potential suitors.

A competent attorney's main goal should be to appeal to the jury's emotions. As with crowds in general, this means that they should argue less or just use basic logic. The course of action to be taken has been clearly laid out by an English lawyer who is well-known for his victories in the assize courts: —

"He would watch the jurors intently while he made his appeal. The best possible chance has arrived. Because of his knowledge and expertise, the attorney is able to discern the impact of each word on the jurors' faces and makes inferences accordingly. He starts by determining which jurors are already in favor of his position. After a brief period of labor to secure their adherence, he focuses on the members who appear to be unfriendly toward the accused and looks for the reason behind their opposition. This is the tricky part of his work because, aside from the sense of fairness, there are a gazillion reasons to condemn a guy."

These few sentences recapitulate the entire process of the art of oratory, and we can understand why a speech that has been planned in advance has such a little impact — it is important to be able to adjust the language used on the fly to suit the impression that is created.

The speaker does not have to persuade every juror to agree with him; rather, only the most influential members will decide the jury's overall verdict. Similar to any group, juries consist of a select few persons who act as mentors to the others. The aforementioned attorney states, "I have found from experience that one or two energetic men suffice to carry the rest of the jury with them." It is up to you to persuade those two or three with deft ideas. Above everything, and above all, you have to make them happy. The man who is a member of the group that you have managed to win over is almost certain,

It is often known that Lachaud never lost sight of the two or three jurymen who he perceived to be powerful yet unyielding during any of the remarks he would give during an assize session. He was generally effective in persuading these uncooperative jurors. However, he once had to deal with a juryman in the provinces, whom he tried to convince of anything for three-quarters of an hour using only the shrewdest of arguments; the man was the seventh juryman, the first on the second bench. The situation was hopeless.

Chachard abruptly halted his fervent protest in the middle of it and asked the court president, "Would you give instructions for the curtain there in front?"

A number of writers, including some of the most eminent, have recently launched a forceful campaign opposing the jury system, despite the fact that it is our sole defense against the extremely common mistakes made by an unchecked caste.25 Some of these authors support a jury comprised only of members of the enlightened classes; however, we have previously shown that, even in this scenario, the verdicts would be the same as those rendered under the current system. Some authors, taking a stance against the injustices done by jurors, proposed doing away with juries altogether and substituting judges.

It is hard to understand how these purported reformers can ignore the fact that the mistakes the jury is accused of making were made.

Being well-versed in both the psychology of castes and other types of crowds, I cannot think of a single instance in which, having been falsely accused of a crime, I would not sooner deal with a jury than with magistrates. There should be a possibility that the former would acknowledge my innocence, but there should be very little probability that the latter would do the same. One should be afraid of the power of crowds, but one should be even more afraid of the power of certain castes. Castes are seldom receptive to conviction, whereas crowds are.

13

Chapter IV.

Electoral Crowds

CHAPTER IV.

The general traits of electoral crowds; how to persuade them; the attributes that a candidate should have; the necessity of prestige; the reason why working-class and peasant voters so rarely select candidates from their own class; the impact of words and formulas on voters; the general nature of election oratory; the formation of voters' opinions; the power of political committees; their representation of the most blatant form of tyranny; the committees of the Revolution; Despite its little psychological significance, universal suffrage cannot be substituted. It expresses what all nations agree upon and explains why the votes cast would still be the same even if just a small class of residents were granted the ability to vote.

Electoral crowds, or collectivities endowed with the authority to choose representatives for specific positions, are heterogeneous assemblies; however, because their actions are limited to selecting amongst candidates, they exhibit only a limited number of the previously mentioned attributes. Among the traits unique to crowds, they exhibit a specific, albeit minor, capability for thinking, as well as impatience, credulous, simplicity, and the lack of a critical spirit. Furthermore, it is possible to track the role that affirmation, repetition, prestige, and contagion — as well as the impact of crowd leaders — played in their choice.

Let's look at the strategies to be used to convince voters. Their approaches will make it easier to infer their psychology.

The candidate's prestige is the most crucial need.

Only wealth-derived status may really supplant personal prestige. Even brilliance and talent are not very significant predictors of success.

However, the need that the candidate have prestige — that is, the ability to impose himself on the people without debate — is crucial. It is because such a person has little respect among the electors — of whom the majority are working men or peasants — that they so seldom pick a guy from their own ranks to represent them. If they do, by chance, elect a guy who is comparable to them, it's usually for incidental motives, like retaliating against a notable individual,

The candidate should avoid making too many generalizations in his written platform as this might be used against him in the future by his opponents; on the other hand, he should not exaggerate too much in his speech. The most significant improvements could be boldly pledged. These exaggerations, as they currently stand, have a significant impact but are not legally binding. It is a persistent observation that voters never bother to inquire about the extent to which the candidate they have returned has adhered to the platform they have supported and on which they believed victory in the election would have been assured.

Each of the previously discussed persuasion aspects must be acknowledged in the material that follows.

"To appease the radicals who have realized that a centralized republic is really a monarchy under cover, Cortes overwhelmingly declared a federal republic, even though not a single voter could articulate the meaning of what they had just cast their ballots for. However, this mixture made everyone exceedingly happy; the dizzying, intoxicated euphoria was felt by everybody. On earth, a new era of decency and pleasure had just begun. A Republican felt he had been gravely humiliated when his opponent denied him the designation of federalist. In the streets, people shouted, "Long live the federal republic!" to one another. Following that, the army's lack of discipline and its troops' independence were praised for its mystic qualities.

Regarding the potential impact of argumentation on voters'

CHAPTER IV.

thoughts, the only reason someone might have the slightest doubt about this is if they have never perused the minutes of an electioneering meeting. Affirmations, insults, and even physical violence are exchanged at such a gathering, yet arguments are never had. If there is a reason for the brief pause, it is because one of the attendees, who has a reputation for being a "tough customer," has indicated that he is going to heckle the candidate by asking him one of those humiliating questions that usually make the audience laugh. The opposing party's happiness, though, is fleeting since the questioner's voice is quickly overpowered by the clamor raised by his opponents.

"The Allemanist party arranged a fantastic gathering last evening in the Hall of Commerce, located on Rue du Faubourg-du-Temple. This was a prelude to the workers' fiesta on May 1st. The meeting's catchphrase was "Calm and Tranquillity." Comrade G— — makes references to socialists as "humbugs" and "idiots." "An exchange of insults occurs at this point, and speakers and audience members start fighting. Tables, benches, and chairs are turned into weapons," &c., &c.

It is unimaginable to think for a second that this conversation description is exclusive to a particular class of electors and contingent on their social standing. No matter if the attendees in an anonymous assembly are just highly educated individuals, the nature of the conversation is always the same.

"As the evening wore on, the chaos only got worse; I don't think any speaker was able to say more than two phrases without getting cut off. Shouts erupted from all directions at once, or from this way and that direction at random. There was a mixture of cheers and hisses, aggressive arguments taking place amongst audience members, people brandishing sticks menacingly, others beating a tattoo on the ground, and cries of "Let him speak!" and "Put him out!" were directed at those who interrupted.

"M. C— — lavished such epithets as odious and cowardly, monstrous, vile, venal and vindictive, on the Association, which he declared he wanted to destroy," &c., etc.

One may wonder how an elector could possibly form an opinion under such circumstances. It is an odd illusion about the amount of liberty that a collectivity may enjoy to pose such a question. Although opinions are pushed upon them, crowds seldom take pride in having well-reasoned opinions. The election committees, whose leading lights are often publicans, control the attitudes and votes of the electors in the case at hand. They have significant power over the working class, whom they give credit to. Are you aware .

This is how election crowd psychology works. It is neither better nor worse than that of other crowds. As a result, I do not infer anything against universal suffrage from the above information. If I were to decide its fate, I would keep it exactly as is for pragmatic reasons — reasons that can really be inferred from our study of crowd psychology. I'll go ahead and provide them based on this.

Undoubtedly, the drawbacks of universal suffrage are too evident to be ignored. It is certain that a tiny number of exceptionally intelligent people have contributed to civilization. These individuals are the pinnacle of a pyramid, whose phases correspond to a decline in mental capacity.

Furthermore, because this doctrine appears to be rational, trying to refute it would be even less fruitful.

"In an era of equality," Tocqueville rightly points out, "men have no faith in each other on account of their being all alike; yet this same similitude gives them an almost limitless confidence

CHAPTER IV.

in the judgment of the public, the reason being that it does not appear probable that, all men being equally enlightened, truth and numerical superiority should not go hand in hand."

Is it really thought that a limited right to vote, limited to those who possess the necessary cognitive abilities, will lead to an enhancement in the collective decision-making of voters?

As a result, the votes cast today would be same if the electorate were made up only of people who were well educated in the sciences. Their feelings and the mood of the celebration would mostly serve as their guides. We shouldn't be spared any of the challenges we face now, and the harsh caste system should undoubtedly be imposed upon us.

The right to vote for the masses, whether it be limited or universal, practiced under a republic or a monarchy, in France, Belgium, Greece, Portugal, or Spain, is universal and, at its core, represents the unspoken needs and desires of the human race.

14

Chapter V.

Parliamentary

The majority of traits shared by diverse, non-anonymous audiences are also evident in parliamentary assemblies: the simplicity of their beliefs; their suggestibility and its bounds; their unwavering, unchanging beliefs; and the cause of the preponderance of hesitation. The position of the leaders — The basis for their notoriety — They are the real rulers of an assembly, and as such, their votes are only those of a tiny minority — The total authority they wield — The components of their artful oratory — Words and pictures — The psychological need that the leaders have to generally be narrow-minded and obstinate in their beliefs — Speakers without status can never get attention for their ideas; assemblies' exaggerated feelings, whether positive or negative; at some point, these feelings become instinctive; the meetings

CHAPTER V.

Parliamentary assemblies serve as an example of diverse, non-identifiable audiences. Despite the fact that its members are elected in different ways throughout history and throughout countries, they have a lot of traits. In this instance, race has an effect that tends to accentuate or lessen the traits typical of crowds, but not to stop them from occurring. The parliamentary assemblies of the most dissimilar nations — Greece, Italy, Portugal, Spain, France, and America — present striking parallels in their discussions and voting, leaving the corresponding administrations to deal with similar challenges.

Furthermore, the parliamentary system embodies the goal of all contemporary civilized societies.

One of their most crucial traits, in their perspective, is simplicity. In the case of both parties, and particularly with regard to the Latino population, such crowds invariably have the inclination to solve the most complex societal problems using the most basic abstract ideas and universal rules. The party's guiding ideas naturally differ from one another, but because each member is a part of a larger group, they are always more likely to overstate the significance of their beliefs and take them to the farthest extent possible.

Parliaments so tend to be particularly reflective of extreme viewpoints. The best illustration of the clever simplification of viewpoints particular to assembly is provided.

Every member of an assembly has firm beliefs that are unwavering notwithstanding endless debate on any topic of local or regional importance. When it comes to issues like protection or the right to distill alcohol, when the interests of powerful electors are at stake, even the greatest Demosthenes could not sway a deputy's vote.

The recommendations made by these voters, which were received prior to voting day, are substantially more than recommendations from any other source in order to nullify them and preserve a completely fixed view.27 There is no longer any fixedity of view on broad issues like toppling a Cabinet or imposing a tax, and leaders' ideas can have an impact, but not in precisely the same way.

The same rationale underlies the fact that each returning chamber contains both very variable and highly steady opinions. Overall, because broad questions are more common, there is a lot of hesitation in the Chamber. This indecision stems from the electorate's constant anxiety, whose suggestions are constantly latent and tend to offset the leaders' effect.

However, in those endless debates about topics on which the participants in an assembly lack strongly held prior notions, the leaders are unquestionably the experts. The fact that these leaders are present in assemblies around the nation in their capacity as heads of organizations makes their necessity obvious.

In his observations on the notable members of the Assembly

CHAPTER V.

of 1848, of which he was a part, M. Jules Simon provides us with some quite intriguing instances of the fact that the reputation of these political leaders is unique and unrelated to name or celebrity: — "Two months before he was all-powerful, Louis Napoleon was entirely without the least importance." Mounting the tribune was Victor Hugo. He was not successful.

He received the same amount of attention as Felix Pyat, but not as much acclaim. Vaulabelle told me about Felix Pyat, saying, "I don't like his ideas, but he is one of the greatest writers and the greatest orator in France." Despite having a remarkable and strong mind,

The previous section was relatively lacking in psychology, therefore I have quoted it only for the data it presents, not the explanations. If a crowd started giving credit to its leaders for their efforts, whether they were party-related or served their nation, they would instantly lose their identity as a crowd. The masses that follow a leader because of his reputation are influenced by him, not because they are motivated by interest or appreciation.

As a result, the leader who enjoys enough prestige has practically total authority. The enormous impact that a renowned deputy who was defeated in the most recent general election due to specific financial circumstances exercised over a protracted period of years, owing to his fame, is widely known.

"The main reason we paid three times as much as we should have for Tonkin, why we stayed on shaky ground in Madagascar for so long, why we were cheated out of an empire in the Lower Niger region, and why we no longer hold the dominant position we once held in Egypt is all due to M. X. We have lost more territory to M. X— —'s ideas than to Napoleon I's catastrophes."

We shouldn't have a particularly sour vengeance toward the

concerned leader. It is evident that he has come at a huge expense to us, but he gained a lot of power by following popular opinion, which in colonial affairs was not at all what it is now. A leader nearly always follows public opinion and propagates all of its faults; he is rarely ahead of the curve.

Aside from their stature, the leaders we are dealing with can be persuaded by the elements we have previously listed several times. A leader has to have grasped these resources, at least in part, in order to employ them skillfully.

The "striking terms" mentioned in the preceding quotation cannot be given too much weight. We have already emphasized several times the unique power of words and formulae. They have to be picked such that they conjure up really clear pictures. The sentence that follows, which is taken from a speech given by one of our assembly leaders, is a great illustration: —

"When the same vessel shall bear away to the fever-haunted lands of our penitentiary settlements the politician of shady reputation and the anarchist guilty of murder, the pair will be able to converse together, and they will appear to each other as the two complementary aspects of one and the same state of society."

As a result, the speaker's enemies all felt threatened by the extremely vivid vision that was conjured up. They imagined a dual picture of the fever-stricken nation and the ship that may take them away. After all, could it be that they fall under the vague heading of "political threats"? They felt the underlying terror that the members of the Convention must have felt, anxiety that made them always submit to Robespierre when he threatened them with the guillotine in his ambiguous remarks. The leaders have every incentive to engage in the most absurd exaggerations. The speaker whose statement I just mentioned was able to state without inciting violent protests,

While a leader may occasionally possess great intelligence and education, these attributes often work against them. The intensity and ferocity of belief that apostles require is much blunted by intellect, which always makes its possessor indulgent by demonstrating the complexity of things, permitting explanation, and fostering comprehension. The most influential crowd leaders throughout history, including those of the Revolution, have regrettably had quite limited intellectual horizons. Conversely, individuals with the most limited intelligence have also had the most impact.

The most well-known of them, Robespierre, often astounds listeners with his speeches since they are so illogical that it is impossible to find a reasonable explanation by reading them.

The cliches and repetitions of Latin culture and pedagogical eloquence serve to foster a mentality that is more childlike than sophisticated, with concepts of attack and defense restricted to schoolboys' belligerent demeanor. Not a concept, not a charming phrase, not a memorable hit: a tirade of cries that bores us. After finishing this dull reading, one is inclined to say, "Oh!" with the charming Camille Desmoulins."

Sometimes it is awful to consider the influence that a guy with status may have when his extreme narrow-mindedness and strong convictions are coupled. These requirements must be met, however, in order for a guy to disregard setbacks and exhibit an extreme degree of willpower. Men with conviction and enthusiasm are the masters that crowds naturally recognize as being the ones they need most.

The speaker's reputation virtually entirely determines the outcome of a speech in a parliamentary assembly, not the arguments he makes. The strongest evidence for this is the fact that when a speaker loses his reputation for any reason, he also loses all of his power and influence.

"When he takes his place in the tribune he draws a document from his portfolio, spreads it out methodically before him, and makes a start with assurance." He boasts to himself that he will instill in his listeners the same sense of conviction that drives him. He is certain he will persuade his audience since he has carefully considered and reweighed his arguments and is well-prepared with numbers and evidence. Any opposition would be pointless in the face of the facts he is about to provide. He starts off with confidence in the righteousness of his cause and the support of his colleagues, who are naturally just concerned with supporting the truth.

Parliamentary assemblies have the distinct quality of always being extremely passionate when they reach a certain level of intensity, at which point they resemble regular, motley crowds. They will be perceived as having either the worst excesses or the greatest deeds of bravery. The person is no longer himself, and as a result, he will vote against policies that are most detrimental to his own interests.

The French Revolutionary War demonstrates the degree to which groups may become unconscious of themselves and accept ideas that go counter to their own interests. The nobility made a great sacrifice by giving up its rights, but on a historic night during the Constituent Assembly sessions, it did so without hesitation.

According to Taine, "they accepted and decreed acts which they held in horror — measures which were not merely stupid and dumb, but crimes — the death of their friends and innocent individuals.

Danton, the Revolution's natural leader and brilliant booster,

CHAPTER V.

was overwhelmingly dispatched to the scaffold by the Left, with enthusiastic cheers from the Right. The Left supports the Right in unanimity as they vote for the harshest laws of the revolutionary administration, receiving the loudest cheers in the process. The Convention, through spontaneous and repeated re-elections, unanimously and amid cheers of praise and fervor, amid expressions of intense sympathy for Collot d'Herbois, Couthon, and Robespierre, maintains in power the homicidal government that the Plain detests for being homicidal, and the Mountain detests.

"The divides, suspicions, jealousies, naive confidence, and unending dreams of the Republican party ultimately led to its downfall. Its widespread distrust was the only thing that matched its cunning and candor. The peasant and the kid have the same feeling of terrors and illusions, as well as an absence of any sense of legality and grasp of discipline. Their aggressiveness is equal to their docility, and their calmness is equal to their impatience. This disorder is a natural result of both a lack of knowledge and an unformed temperament. Such people are not surprised by anything, and they find everything upsetting. Shaking with terror or courageous to the brink of bravery, they would encounter fire and water.

Thankfully, not every one of the qualities that have just been mentioned as necessary for legislative assemblies is always present. These gatherings only qualify as crowds during specific times. Most of the time, the people who make them still maintain their uniqueness, which explains how an assembly may produce very good technical legislation. It is true that these laws were written by a professional who worked alone in his study to create them, and that the legislation that was voted on was actually the result of an individual rather than an assembly.

These laws are the finest by nature.

They won't become devastating until a number of changes have transformed them into the product of a collective.

Parliamentary assemblies are the greatest form of governance that humanity has yet developed, despite all the challenges that come with operating them. More importantly, though, they are the finest way for mankind to break free from the shackles of individual tyranny. For all individuals who make up the elite of a civilization — philosophers, intellectuals, authors, artists, and knowledgeable men, in other words — they unquestionably make up the ideal form of governance.

Furthermore, there are actually only two major risks associated with them: the first is the unavoidable wastage of money, and the second is the gradual infringement of personal freedom. The first of these risks is a necessary byproduct of the electoral masses' haste and lack of vision.

Although it may not be as evident, the second of the above-mentioned dangers — the unavoidable limitations on liberty brought about by legislative assemblies — is still quite real. It is the outcome of the countless laws — each with a limiting action — for which parliaments feel obligated to vote and whose repercussions cause them to be mostly blind due to their short-sightedness.

Since even England, which undoubtedly offers the most popular kind of parliamentary regime — one in which the representative is most independent of his electorate — has been unable to avoid it, the threat must be quite real. In a book that is already very old, Herbert Spencer demonstrated that a rise in perceived liberty inevitably leads to a fall in genuine liberty.

"As I mentioned before, legislation has followed the path at this time. Dictatorial policies that proliferate quickly have a tendency to limit individual liberty in two ways. More and more regulations are being created each year, restricting the citizen in areas where his actions were previously entirely free and compelling him to carry out tasks that he was previously free to perform or not perform as he pleased. Simultaneously, increasing public, particularly local, burdens have further curtailed his freedom by reducing the amount of his earnings that he can allocate as he pleases and increasing the amount that is taken from him to be used in accordance with the public authorities' good will."

Herbert Spencer has not mentioned one particular way that this progressive restriction of liberties manifests itself in every nation: the enactment of these numerous legislative measures, which all function as restrictive orders in general, inevitably increases the number, authority, and influence of the bureaucrats tasked with carrying them out. In this sense, these bureaucrats frequently rise to the position of actual rulers in developed nations. The administrative caste is the only group that is unaffected by the constant shifting of power and is known for its irresponsibility, impersonality, and perpetuity. This gives them even more power. Nothing embodies an oppressive tyranny more than the one that exists under.

Once reaching this stage, the person is obligated to look outside of himself for the forces he is no longer able to locate inside himself. Governmental activities always expand in tandem with the population' growing powerlessness and disinterest. They are the ones who must unavoidably display the initiative, sense of adventure, and leadership that private individuals lack. They have the responsibility to manage everything, oversee everything, and keep everything safe. The State turns into an all-knowing deity. Experience however demonstrates that the strength and durability of such gods' power was never particularly great.

In the case of certain peoples, this gradual restriction of all rights, notwithstanding an external license that gives them the impression that these liberties are still theirs,

What do we observe if we look at the primary lines that explain the rise to prominence and decline of the civilizations that came before our own?

A vast group of persons from different backgrounds came together during the beginning of civilization due to opportunities for migration, invasion, and conquest. The only thing that unites these guys, despite having various bloodlines, dialects, and beliefs, is the partially acknowledged law of a chief. These disorganized groups exhibit many of the psychological traits associated with crowds. They possess the ephemeral unity of throngs, as well as courage, frailty, impatience, and violence. Regarding them, nothing is stable. They are nomadic people. eventually completes its task.

It is possible that at this point a new civilization with its institutions, values, and artistic creations may emerge. The race will gradually gain the attributes required to give it splendor, vigor, and grandeur as it strives toward its goal. Undoubtedly, there will still be crowds at times, but underneath their ephemeral and shifting qualities lies a stable foundation — the collective intelligence of the race that controls the course of events and restricts the nation's changes. Time starts its destructive operation once it has completed its creation deed, from which neither gods nor humans can escape. A civilization is doomed when it reaches a certain point of power and complexity and then stops growing.

The race gradually loses the characteristics that gave it cohe-

CHAPTER V.

siveness, unity, and power as its ideal gradually fades. Individuals may become more intelligent and have stronger personalities, but this racial egoism is being replaced by an excessive development of personal egoism, which is accompanied by a decline in character and a reduced ability to take action. In the end, what was once a people, a unity, and a whole dissolves into a collection of disjointed individuals that are momentarily kept together by the traditions and institutions of the group. Men are now divided by their goals and interests and unable to control themselves, therefore they must direct in their smallest ways. A people's life cycle is to transition from the barbaric to the civilized condition in pursuit of an ideal, and then, when this ideal has lost its worth, to deteriorate and perish.

WRITTEN BY:
Dwight Howe

Thank you
THE END

www.ingramcontent.com/pod-product-compliance
Lightning Source LLC
LaVergne TN
LVHW011955070526
838202LV00054B/4926